Ulrike Dietmann

ON THE WINGS OF HORSES

A Hero's Journey into the Heart of the Creature

A Book for You

Foreword by Linda Kohanov
Cover Art © Kim McElroy

© *English edition: 2012 Ulrike Dietmann*

Original title: "Auf den Flügeln der Pferde – eine Heldinnenreise ins Herz der Kreatur" © *2010, Wu Wei Verlag, Isabella Sonntag, www.wu-wei-verlag.com*

Translated by: Andrea Zwingelberg-Woods and Roy Woods

Publisher: spiritbooks, Kirchheim/Teck, www.spiritbooks.de

ISBN: 978-3-9815421-4-1

Cover image: Cover Art "King Midas" © *Kim McElroy, spiritofhorse.com*

Cover design: Antje Stephan www.epona-spirit.de

Publishing services: www.tredition.de

Printed in Germany

Translated
by
Andrea Zwingelberg-Woods
and
Roy Woods

For the shining stars in my life
Martin, Lea, Joel

Some things, we know deep in our soul,
are true, no matter what anybody may say about them.

Shelley Rosenberg, horse trainer

Important tip: The methods introduced here are no substitute for an education in riding or handling horses. Neither the author nor the publishing company will take any responsibility for results which originate directly or indirectly from reading this book.

Foreword by Linda Kohanov

How often do we read about the mythic or historical adventures of heroes, barely noticing the silent heroes they ride? What is a hero, after all? Someone who transcends survival instincts to face the unknown, sometimes enduring terrifying ordeals for a greater cause? Someone who remains poised in the midst of turmoil, who prevails despite the odds to capture a treasure from the gods, an uplifting innovation, enduring significant hardships to bring some glistening piece of magic back to the tribe?

By this definition, horses are every bit as heroic as their riders, perhaps even more so. For thousands of years, pioneers faced considerable hardships as they explored the world on horseback, charting territory they would have struggled to traverse on foot, reveling in a primal experience of freedom, strength, and speed so exhilarating that we still measure our most sophisticated engines in units of horse power.

Warriors, carried by their loyal mounts, fought with swords, spears, and arrows, later enduring musket and cannon fire. That men could be persuaded to stare death in the face like this is one thing. But riding a *prey* animal, a vegetarian, a species that much prefers flight over fight, anywhere near the scent of blood---let alone the din of absolute chaos and unmitigated agony---goes against every hard-wired impulse the horse possesses. If, as scientists once insisted, animals are machines programmed for survival, ruled exclusively by instinct, such an act would be impossible.

In the twenty-first century, of course, increasing research supports our experience that animals are sentient beings with an incredible capacity to feel, learn, love, and even perform altruistic acts. Those of us who work with horses in the fields of equine-facilitated learning and therapy, however, see something even more miraculous happening. Horses are teaching people how to be better leaders, parents, spouses, companions, and innovators. Whether or not we literally climb on the backs of these powerful, soulful beings, horses uplift us, filling us with courage, awe, wonder, and delight, sometimes awakening gifts we didn't know we had.

For many equestrians, this happens accidentally as they prepare for a show or take a trail ride. But what if we purposefully tap the horse's ability to make us better humans?

Ulrike Dietmann offers a heartwarming, empowering program for doing just that. In this book, she uses the model of the hero's journey, developed by the late author and mythologist Joseph Campbell, helping us consciously, and thereby much more efficiently, access what horses have been silently teaching riders, heroes, pioneers, leaders, and artists for millennia. Her graceful, intelligent writing is also clear and easy to understand as she makes some normally complex personal development principles surprisingly accessible.

Horses are incredible teachers, but they need good translators to bring their wisdom to a wider human audience. Ulrike is a great translator of horse wisdom. Read this book, follow the activities, and answer the poignant, perceptive questions she asks, and I promise you, your life will change. You will become the hero of your own unique story, and you will realize once and for all, that, even when you wander off the main trail and get lost in the woods, you're never alone in this world. Every heroic journey is a partnership between the rider and her horse.

Linda Kohanov, Author of *The Tao of Equus, Riding between the Worlds, Way of the Horse,* and *The Power of the Herd*

The preface is important

If you want to profit personally from this book, I suggest you read the preface first, because here you will discover how best to work with the book.

This is a very personal journey into areas of your feelings and your consciousness which you may not have entered before. I will guide you on this journey, but you must take the individual steps yourself.

There is only ever *one* first reading of a book and that first reading will have the strongest effect. Therefore, I advise you to read the chapters one after another and to carry out the tasks as you read each respective chapter. The book takes the form of a journey in which each step is based on the previous ones.

If you first leaf through the book to see what to expect, you will approach it later with a more guarded attitude and forfeit some of the opportunities the journey offers. Clearly it is your decision, I just want you to be forewarned.

The book adopts the formula of a hero's journey.

What is the hero's journey?

The hero's journey is a mythological model developed by the world-renowned mythologist Joseph Campbell. He discovered this structure by questioning what all stories, in all cultures and at all times have in common. The hero's journey is a venture into the unconscious to attain insight and personal growth.

It is a valuable model to describe the special experiences people can have if they connect with horses in an authentic way.

The heroic journey applies both to ancient and archaic myths as well as to Hollywood movies. Hollywood often uses the heroic journey model in developing screenplays. The first blockbuster film developed in this way was *Starwars* by George Lucas. A film like *Pretty Woman* also embodies the structure of the heroic journey.

But this is not our concern here, I merely wanted to give you some information on the background. It was through my work as a scriptwriter that I became acquainted with the hero's journey and since then have applied it to everything I write. For many years I have also been teaching the hero's journey.

I have tested the journey in all its conceivable variations and have continuously had excellent results with it. It is a key not only to story narrative, but also a key to being.

After I learnt to communicate with horses, and to work with them in a completely new way, I wondered whether the heroic journey could also provide a model for capturing these elusive experiences. My answer was to write this book.

My work with horses was inspired by Linda Kohanov's books and the Epona Approach which she developed in cooperation with other innovative horse people. I have learnt the Epona Approach and I work as an Eponaquest Advanced Instructor in Germany and worldwide. I teach the Hero's Journey based on the Epona Approach and offer my own Apprenticeship as a Hero's Journey Instructor.

The basic idea of this approach is that it is not in fact the horse that must change, but the human being. Only then is true communication with a horse possible, only when the person becomes what he or she really is: a creature of nature, a creature which strives for love, for connection and for development like all living beings.

Horses can be our guides on this path. The hero's journey connects the ancient myths of the gods and goddesses, priests and priestesses, male and female shamans with the modern stories of our civilization which are based on our individual psychology. The hero's journey incorporates both contemporary people and primeval initiates. One thing above all else happens on this journey: we draw closer to what horses really have to tell us and teach us. And through contact with horses our perception of all creation and of ourselves changes. We become what we have always been: natural human beings.

Different models of the hero's journey exist, all of which, however, follow the same basic principle: the growth of personality by confronting our shadow. This can be painful, but ultimately brings forth healing.

This book, then, will contribute to your personal growth and to your better understanding of horses, and to a harmonious relationship with these remarkable creatures. Whether you are a horse owner or leisure rider, whether you work professionally with horses or simply feel drawn to these beautiful creatures, you will profit in your own personal way from this book.

Each chapter deals with one step of the journey. Each step has its own content and tasks. You will find a summary of the tasks at the end of the book.

With every step there are several tasks to work on. Your answers and discoveries will coalesce to form a larger picture and a wider perspective.

The tasks are marked in bold type. You can work on them while reading the individual chapters, wait till the end of the chapter, or if you prefer: wait till you have finished reading the book as a whole.

The essence of a journey is progression. It is not so much a question of reaching a goal but of taking the individual steps. And yet there is a broader framework within which everything finds its place. Behind each step there is an order which relates all the parts to each other and imbues them with meaning.

You can trust the dynamics of the hero's journey to carry you forwards. Therefore it is important that you take each step at a time and in the right sequence. If you change the order, you will reach a different result.

In each chapter you will discover the significance of the individual steps. I will recount events which I myself have experienced as well as stories I have been told by others whose credibility I have verified. In some stories I have combined different incidents to form a single story in order to clarify the meaning. In many cases I have changed the names of the persons involved to protect their identity. Furthermore you will learn about the background of intuitive communication with horses, about how to find true relationship and gain access to the wisdom and healing power of nature.

I recommend that you write a journal while you are working on the tasks, so as to put your thoughts in order and to gain an overview of your development. You can also draw or paint or choose any other form of expression you feel comfortable with. You do not have to fulfill all the tasks meticulously. Select what appeals to you. Feel quite free to follow your own intuition and inspiration.

Don't try to be perfect, just be honest with yourself. This is quite enough.

I wish you a wonderful journey

Ulrike

Step One
Who Are You?

None of this means anything. This is not reality, I think as I sit with my eyes closed, being carried along by a horse. What I consider to be my world, the perceptible world, is just a segment of a larger whole. My familiar world drops off me like an old skin and underneath it something new, something tempting opens up. Temptation and raging fear alternate. What is happening to me? My whole body is trembling, while the horse beneath me rocks like a boat on the high seas.

In the sky the seagulls from the sea nearby are shrieking, they tear open the air, a noise which echoes in my legs, arms and above all my chest where the battle takes place between remaining in control and letting go. Between clinging to the familiar world and letting go. Am I losing my mind?

The images come, they come more and more frequently and faster. I am wrapped in the warm fur of tiredness, and the rocking of the horse's body calms me. But suddenly not even the horse gives me any security any more. At the same time as a new wave of fear floods over me, my grip on the horse falters.

The 'Journey Ride', a guided ride on a horse's back, requires that I keep my eyes closed. My thighs tense up as if I was sitting on a horse for the first time.

What I once knew, what I was able to do, who I was, all this has dissolved. In my inner eye the image of an Arabian horse appears, its eyes wide with fear–and I feel very vulnerable.

I have always been like that: defenseless. I was just not aware of it.

Only now do I know that not a breath, not a blink of the eyes, not a swish of my horse's tail occurs without it finding a place in some inexplicable order. I hear the horse sigh. It is his way of telling me that he shares my opinion.

It is the moment when everything begins, when I begin to perceive my world not just with my mind, but with my heart, my body, my whole being. The moment when the horses takes me with them on a journey, an adventure starts which is as old as mankind, and which threatens to be forgotten in our contemporary civilization. A journey into the heart of creation, into the heart of everything living, into the heart of the creature. A million-year-old journey which begins anew again and again, with every living creature that is born.

The sun must have pushed through the bunched clouds. Its warmth strokes my face, warms my shoulders and something in me shifts. I have accepted my fear, the gelding's sighs have calmed me down, he is here, I feel it and through him I am also here. My thighs relax, I have arrived here on the horse's back.

I ask my horse partner: Am I destined to be a spiritual author–whatever that may mean? The term *spiritual* has not been part of my vocabulary up to now. And neither do I know where the question suddenly comes from. And even less: where it will lead me. Up to now I have been an author of horse fiction, of romantic novels and commercial texts.

His name is Ambrose. He sends me the picture of a universe sprinkled with countless stars. I nod. This is your source, Ambrose adds. The source of all creativity. I think writing is spiritual by nature because it is creative and because all creativity arises from a world beyond what is conceivable. And not only all creativity but everything living is fed by two worlds, from this world and that, the known and the hidden worlds which I am just getting to know.

You will find many sources of inspiration, says Ambrose. It is strange that a horse is talking to me. Or maybe not. It is only strange from my old, limited viewpoint. Ambrose does not seem to find it in the least strange. For him it seems to be the most natural thing in the world. I like this new perspective.

The image of the star-spangled universe changes into the steppes. That I see these images seems to me to be completely normal, and at the same time I know that Ambrose is sending them to me. I see a valley with gently rising hills which fades into eternity, a basin curving gently inwards with the wind blowing through it. The grass sways as if stroked by a hand. It is yellow and dried up and the hooves sink silently into it.

Now my fear has completely disappeared. That is how we go through life, says Ambrose, you and I, free and yet connected. Not only now but always. Our soul is always here, in the place where freedom dwells, the place where we are at one.

What else have you got for me? The universe, the steppes ... Is it presumptuous to ask for even more? Come on, Ambrose replies, where did you get that from? Who says that wisdom, love, communication only come in small doses?—I think only humans can come up with something like that.

The journey continues. Ambrose shows me a golden chalice. The sun is rising over the edge of it. I stand with the chalice in my hand before the spreading flood of light and I grin about something incomprehensible which rises in me like the glowing sun. I am completely filled by this light which floods my body and releases a barely describable feeling of well-being.

The horse continues to rock beneath me, but I now feel I am in complete communion with him. The border between Ambrose's body and mine dissolves. I feel his muscles, I feel how he lifts his legs, I feel how relaxed he is as he walks. I should always ride like this. This is the way to sit: the true rider's seat.

The golden chalice.

What does it mean, I ask Ambrose. The very moment I ask the question, I have the answer.

The chalice is the universal vessel, it stands for everything. For the soul, for creation, for the world we live in. The chalice stands for the light which becomes form. It is the original form from which all else arises. It can become everything, god, goddess, art, knowledge. I think of the cornucopias on the illustrations of the old goddesses, think of the Holy Grail sought by knights, of the Chalice from the Last Supper of Christianity.

I want to journey on, to know more, because I have gained

access to an inexhaustible source of wisdom. At the same time I become conscious that my journey will not go on forever. Twenty minutes, according to Yvonne Monahan, the workshop facilitator. I am sad that everything will soon be over. I am afraid that maybe I will never again return to this place where there is light and all questions are answered. I want to hold on to this new, unknown world and the more I clutch at it, the more I realize it is fading. It is me who is making it disappear with my doubts and fears. I suddenly think that perhaps I imagined it all. I am just sitting on a horse, I am not even riding, I am being led—and the light I saw is the sun emerging from behind the clouds, penetrating my closed eyelids. The rest was my fevered imagination.

I feel guilty about Ambrose because I am dismissing as nonsense the wisdom which he has shared with me. But how could I ever come up with the idea that a horse could talk to me? I now feel really bad. All the magic has gone. I would prefer to open my eyes, dismount and go home.

How could I ever have spent so much money on a workshop called *Self Discovery through the Way of the Horse,* for which I have flown especially to Ireland? What part of me produced this crazy idea and what on earth did I expect to gain from it?

Now the riding no longer feels so good. The connection to Ambrose is broken, I feel tired and somehow sad. But it is not a genuine feeling, actually, I feel nothing at all. It scares me. Where has the magic world gone which till now had filled me?

The guided ride is over. We dismount, say good-bye to the horses and we each of us have time for ourselves, time to digest the experience.

I feel depressed for the rest of the day. I write down what I have experienced, make a drawing of the chalice and the sun. Once more there is a faint flickering of the feeling. And something remains. Even if I cannot explain how that could work: I am sure that it was Ambrose who shared these things with me. How can I be so sure of that? Well, it was not a monologue that I delivered up there on the horse. A monologue is different.

But if it is really possible for a horse to communicate with a human being–and not only communicate but initiate him into the highest wisdom–what does that imply about our relationship to horses, to animals in general? If it is really true, then my whole world is upside down.

In the bed-and-breakfast that evening with the heart-warming Irish landlady, Mary Buckley, who supplies me with tea, biscuits and sandwiches, I still feel sad. I think it will take years to grasp what has happened, what Ambrose conveyed to me and what the consequences are.

But in fact, before even a year was out, my whole life would be so changed that, looking back, this experience would merely constitute dipping my big toe in cold water. Everything would change, if I would only stop thinking and start feeling instead.

I have been involved for ten years with Joseph Campbell's 'monomyth' model of the hero's journey. I am a writer, inventing stories is my profession. Myths, says Campbell, are the secret opening through which the inexhaustible energy of the cosmos flows into our reality.

The heroic journey is the mega-myth, the great fractal which branches out into an infinite number of ever smaller fractals. The heroic journey is the discovery that all stories, everywhere in the world, at all times have a common structure and core. Presumably the hero's journey was already being told round our ancestors' campfire, after they had returned from the hunt. And we horse people are also on such a journey, even if we are not aware of it.

Even horses …

Yes, horses! They are here to lead us on our journey. That is the present-day heroic journey of horses. Where horses have no longer economic value and we no longer ride them into war or hitch our wagons to them, they are here to carry us into the shadow world. In Germany there are 11 million horse enthusiasts, the number of horses has tripled during the last 35 years. There seem to be a lot of shadow travellers.

Who is the hero before he sets out? This question precedes the beginning of the journey. It marks the first step.

Becoming aware of who I am, today, now, at this moment. Many people find it odd to even ask this question. Who cares? What is this supposed to be good for? Much more often I ask myself what I want, what I can do, or what I must do. But also who I am?

Who are you? Do you have an answer without thinking too much about it?

This is your first task. Write down what comes to mind. Write until you have an answer that you can feel in your body. If you find an answer in your body, it is the right one.

Years ago when I applied for a job at the screen-writing academy in Munich, I was asked to write a self-portrait. I described myself as *somebody who perceives the essential*. For example as I was driving with friends through a dried-up African savannah and our car ran out of petrol, I was the one who had spotted a row of dusty wine bottles by the roadside some way back. Wine bottles in which petrol was sold.

Horses also concentrate on the essentials. On the next mouthful of grass. On quickly driving away a herd member whose muzzle is edging too close. Their lessons are also extremely precise.

Max, a seasoned cowboy from Wyoming, told me, how, when he was young and bursting with testosterone, he was strolling behind his horse and in high jinx kicked up dust with the toe of his boot. The gelding felt that this disturbed his peace of mind, drew back and knocked the ice-cream Max was just enjoying off its cone. The cone itself remained intact and fortunately Max did too. Since then, said Max, his respect for horses had considerably increased. If you ever watch young stallions wrangling, you will be astonished how they go at one another with hooves and teeth flying, yet without seriously injuring each other.

So I am a person with intuitive access to essentials. My strength is in finding safety and orientation.

What is your strength? Take your time and think about it. Find a particular, personal answer, something that distinguishes your character. Ask for a feeling. If you want, you can use the following examples as stimuli:

Cheerfulness, gratitude, calmness, contentment, self-confidence, friendliness, the gift of loving, clarity, curiosity, resilience, liveliness, enthusiasm, energy, fulfillment, peace-

fulness, gentleness, empathy … Where do you stand in life now, before you begin your journey with horses at your side?

Lisa, when she first opened a picture book entitled *My Little Farm*, had not seen much of the world, apart from the walls of her nursery, the park and the playground. But her eyes sparkled when she discovered it and her finger pointed at the gee-gee. Maybe she already knew it, even before she discovered the drawing of the horse with its smiling button eyes, maybe the picture aroused a memory slumbering in her infant soul, an archetypal image, as psychiatrist C. G. Jung says, anchored in the subconscious of all human beings.

What is your experience with horses up to now? How did it begin? Where has it led you? And where do you stand today? What questions do you have for horses and for yourself? Take your journal and jot down a few words or make a drawing.

As a girl I drew horses' heads, hundreds of them, at every opportunity, as if I were drawing the horse into my heart. It was always the same head, that of the Arabian stallion Hadban Enzahi from Marbach, the state-run stud farm of Baden-Württemberg, from a postcard pinned to my bedroom wall. He was the perfect image of my dreams, regardless of whether they were realistic or not. Hadban Enzahi became a part of my life the moment I held the postcard in my hand. At that time Arabian horses were unaffordable, a rich person's luxury, but nonetheless I was planning a stable and a pasture for my Arabian horse, in the meadow at my front door.

It is important to know who you are, before the journey begins. Because afterwards you will never be the same again. I was an author of entertainment fiction and horse novels. Today I run a creative-writing school and hold workshops in intuitive communication with horses in Germany and internationally. What will I be tomorrow?

The British riding instructor Caroline told me about a typical scene she repeatedly observes at her riding stable, a scene that shows quite well where people stand before they set off on the journey with horses:

"A couple enters the stable, the woman has tears in her eyes at the sight of the horses languishing in their stalls. The man willingly takes part in the first riding lessons. They were after all a birthday present for his wife. Every single time I want to shout: no! Go back to your bars and fitness clubs, to your pleasant life. But it would be no use anyway. A few weeks later the husband gives up the riding lessons, he has more important things to do. He comes once again when there is talk of purchasing a horse. No, I want to shout, but it would be no use anyway. Things take their course. One evening a few months later I see lights still on in the stable. I creep away, so that nobody hears me. From a stall at one end of the stable I hear a woman crying quietly, pouring out her heart to her horse. From then on it is not long before divorce is on the cards. It is like a divine law."

Another story happened to lively Joanne who worked in public relations and was managing a film star.

"One day I woke up and quit my job. My new goal was astonishingly clear. I wanted to find the highest truth that our modern world has to offer. I had never had anything to do with horses, I lived in London, in the midst of its hectic activity. Somebody told me about a woman who rode her horses without bridles or saddles. That was so inconceivable to me that I knew I had to find the answer."

Joanne has given up her former life and is off in search of the wisdom of horses.

An important element of the first step of the heroic journey is not just the question of the heroine's strength but also of her weakness. Strength drives the traveller onwards. Weakness makes her pause, doubt and almost give up.

From the strength, which is only vaguely conscious at the beginning, heroic greatness develops, and from weakness, which at the beginning may only be an undigested memory, a wound develops that splits open, wider and wider, swallowing the seeker's soul as the whale swallows Jonah.

A wound which is larger than a single soul can bear. Let us call it the wound of the creature. It has many faces. One of them is the wound which we inflicted on ourselves when we began to subjugate horses, the favorites of the gods. It is the wound, which man inflicted on the collective body of horses in 6000 years of domestication, the collective memory of these noble creatures, born of the wind. A wound which every foal, born in spring, carries with it and never forgets, even when people treat it ever so carefully and with love.

If a soul awakens to this wound, like those women who come to Caroline's riding stable–it cannot only get to horse people, but to anybody who in an unguarded moment catches the melancholy gaze of a mare–if this wound breaks open, there is no quick cure. It then becomes a very long journey.

27

Some time or other a horse person opens a book and reads. He becomes aware that our civilization arose on the back of the horse. That horses gave us access to the world, made travelling possible, that they carried us through battles and died in uncountable numbers for something completely against their nature. The fact that horses brought kingdoms into existence and caused their downfall. The weak point of all ancient realms was riding, was the ability and inability to connect with horses, to win their support.

A new way of working with horses is in leadership training. Horses build character. You cannot lead a horse either with force or with submissiveness. Leaders of earlier times learnt their leadership from horses. Is this the message from statues of riders in the cities of this world? The horse carries the ruler. The true leader is a horseman.

Today more women than men are involved with horses. Hidden behind this is a revolutionary, historical change which proceeds almost unnoticed. In former cultures women, with virtually no exception, had no access to horses. Today women have chosen horses as partners on their road to self-empowerment—or was it the horses who picked women to finally get their message through to mankind? Because they envisage better chances with women?

When I talk to horse women, we sometimes discuss the subject of spirituality and I am astonished to what degree these women are aware of the spiritual culture we live in. Horses have inspired them to ask all kinds of questions. Our cultural tradition has broken our intimate connection with nature. Animals are subordinate to humans. The skills of animals as companions and teachers are no longer acknowledged. Those who noticed were accused of witchcraft. The witches' love of cats, described as demonic, was nothing but natural communication between creatures. Many animals are seen as symbols of unrestrained sexuality and are thus devalued. Men grin when they hear that a woman loves horse riding. Few can avoid making a suggestive remark. A woman and a stallion: what does that bring to mind?

In Arizona, in Linda Kohanov's Epona Equestrian Center, I participated in a funeral ritual for her beloved stallion, Midnight Merlin. Each of the many women attending expressed their reverence for his natural masculine power, as well as their grief about the way this has been as debased in our society just as feminine power has.

An exception among the Christian saints seems to be Francis of Assisi, who preached to the birds. "All creatures of this earth feel as we do, all creatures of the earth strive for joy, as we do, all creatures of the earth love, suffer and die, as we do, therefore they are equal to us as works of the almighty creator."

A wealthy society lady in a conservative provincial town once said to me: "I don't go to church on Sundays, I go riding. That's my form of worship."

What is your weakness?

Fear of dropping out of a society that does not offer you the security you need? Fear of being different? The fact that you find with horses what you seek in vain from people?

Your vulnerability, your gift of empathy, do you see them as weakness? Your inability to get a grip on your life and to embody what society considers to be a successful person, bursting with energy, efficient, unshakeably self-confident? Your despair about relationships? Your inner emptiness?

Your uncertainty about what to do with your life?

I met Andrea on a ranch in Montana and we became friends. I will use Andrea's words to talk about my weakness:

"In some respects intuitive people are very quiet, even when they talk. It's because they are in a receptive condition, so the receiving channel is always open. I believe people like us feel more like a wild horse. The wildness comes from the fact that we don't know what will happen and who we will become. Because anything can happen, can be said, can be done, when you follow nothing but your intuition. It is not predictable. Most of the time we are involved in receiving, sending and redirecting certain messages. I believe that for outsiders this may seem strange. We simply have this intense connection and are always involved in something."

My weakness is that I quickly feel overwhelmed and unprotected when faced with too many impressions.

As I write this, I feel cold. I am trembling, my body is telling me that I have adopted a vulnerable position. I'm revealing a lot. I could cross out the passage but I won't do that because you, or somebody else, may perhaps find themselves in it, or perhaps you will feel your own vulnerability as you read it. Vulnerability and weakness are unpopular subjects in this society of ours, where we are continually working at being strong and inflexible.

Horses, however, laugh when we trot up to them showing off the kind of strength we have been trained to show. That is not the strength they mean. It is not a genuine strength but an adopted one. In front of horses it fades away like a wisp of smoke from a loud New Year firework. Genuine weakness would be preferable.

Genuine weakness is a good starting point. We have no need to be ashamed of that with horses. Before genuine weakness they incline their noble heads and say: now you are here, now we are friends. This is the whole secret of communicating with horses.

My two cats, Mia and Momo, are lying on their look-out platform as I write this. They are looking in opposite directions, Momo into the room, Mia into the garden. Momo is looking inward, Mia is watching a bird, fascinated. Together they form a picture of that perfect balance between inside and out. I find myself reflected in that and take it as a form of encouragement that I am on the right track with my text.

Animals reflect our internal states. Their behaviour follows an invisible energy. This is something that astonishes me again and again. They make the invisible visible.

Can you describe your weakness? A weakness that runs through your whole life, your development? A weakness that you have observed in yourself in recent days, weeks, months? A weakness that you feel at this very moment?

Can you answer these three questions? Lifelong weakness? Recent weakness? Weakness at this moment? Do you recognize a connection between your answers, a common theme? Take your time looking for the answer or waiting for it–until you have found it.

As you may have already noticed, weakness does not mean achieving something. The question is not whether you are good or bad at swimming, riding, or doing your job. By weakness I mean something personal, a feeling that keeps re-

31

turning, something you do not want to have or a mental habit like weak concentration, flight from reality or the tendency to dominate and trample on others, or act aggressively, uncontrolled.

Maybe you are chronically discontented with yourself, doubt everything, or are bored and indifferent. If you observe yourself for a while, you will find your weakness. Do not search for weaknesses that mean nothing to you, look for a weakness that really hurts or disturbs you. You will recognize a real weakness by feeling it physically.

These are examples for orientation purposes:

Tiredness, exhaustion, depression, indifference, isolation, lethargy, envy, jealousy, vulnerability, loneliness, bitterness, fury, susceptibility to pain, restlessness, a tendency to panic, rage, vengefulness, sadness, despair, timidity, stiffness, humiliation, guilt feelings, inferiority, being driven, susceptibility to stress, tension, confusion, indecisiveness, impatience, disappointment, frustration, irritability ...

If you have developed a feeling for who you are, what your strengths and weaknesses are, you have successfully completed the first stage of the journey.

Do you want to continue on your way? Do we want to make the heroic journey together, each in his or her own way, yet accompanied by all those who are invisible? On the ancient path, which many have walked before us and which leads us into the heart of the creature? Come on then.

Step Two
The Call to Adventure

Joanne, a British woman who quit her well-paid job and set off in search of the highest wisdom of our time, was visiting a horse woman she had heard of on her farm outside London. She saw with her own eyes what seemed to her to be a miracle. The sight of a woman on an unbridled horse raised more questions in her than just those about an unusual style of riding. It stirred her to question the art of how to live her life.

What has that got to do with a horse? How can an animal, which is commonly understood to be limited, and which man, as is well-known, is thought to have to dominate and bully with a bit and a whip, how can it enter into such a trusting relationship with a human being that it voluntarily carries it on its back?

If a horse is prepared to do something like that, am I then, perhaps, also prepared? Prepared no longer to flay myself, force, subdue, control myself, drive and humiliate myself? Describe myself as stupid and limited?

Do I perhaps also deserve to be treated sensitively, empathetically and with understanding? Not only by others, but also by myself? To move without fear, to have confidence, to follow my feelings and impulses, and to feel comfortable in every way? To be creative, to cooperate, to dance, be happy and contented, secure and protected? Not a monster of civilization, but an innocent creature.

According to animal communicator Ted Andrews most people are unaware that they treat themselves the way they treat animals.

Joanne's story depicts a typical call to adventure. It begins with discontentment, a feeling of being unwell, with doubt or curiosity, with an openness to new things–and then suddenly a sentence comes, a message emerges which sets something in motion.

The trigger can be something unimportant and random.

The call to adventure, the heroine's invitation to make the journey, is often woven into a web of events which spreads unnoticed over one's whole life. Many minor events slot together to form a whole. Suddenly doors open, people nod and say "yes" because they sense the underlying current and become part of it themselves.

My call to adventure began like that of many women, while I was leading a life like many other women. I had a family and two children and our next vacation was supposed to take place on a farm. It also turned out that our daughter Lea was in love with horses. For the first time in years I was sitting on a horse again. The memory of going out riding with my grandfather recurred.

None of this would have preoccupied me further, if Hadban Enzahi, the prince, had not returned on one of the rides.

Happiness, psychologists say, is the fulfillment of a childhood dream. A white Arabian flesh-and-blood horse flies up a hill before my eyes with sweeping tail and dancing legs. Something that has long been locked away breaks open. Images and feelings rise up in me from some deep source as if it had never stopped bubbling.

In their own special way horses give humans an identity. My identity revolves around Arabian horses, as strange as that often seems to me. Incredible!

The events unite to form a painting of the senses. My husband had a new job, and we would be moving to a small town in the Black Forest, on the edge of civilization. I would lose my best friend, leave behind my whole life. Recently my literary agent asked me: do you know anything about horses? He was looking for an author to write horse novels. I was more interested in landing a book contract than a horse.

At a horse market I bought a toy horse, supposedly to bring me luck. A contract followed, shortly after that one of four stalls in our riding stable became available. Hadban Enzahi followed, in female form.

The horse had seemed like a dream to me up to the day she was travelling behind me in our transporter on the way to the Black Forest. I played sinking battleships with my daughter–while the previous owner told me straight out that my star-sign was Aquarius.

Since then I have gone through what the Americans call a steep learning curve. The horse was young and had only recently been

35

started. You get what you ask for.

I can precisely pin down the moment of the call to adventure. It was Hadban Enzahi, the forefather, who gave me the sign on that August day on the bank of the river Lech.

Ask any horse owner and he will tell you the moment of his call. His story may perhaps be more dramatic than mine. It does not depend on how dramatic it is but on how effective.

Our life history unceasingly weaves a web of moments until we hear the call, until something inside us responds.

Today it is my task to act as companion to people who have heard the call. I secretly call myself a Spirit Buddy. I like this challenge.

The call comes in countless guises. As a telephone call, a phrase, a picture, a line from a song, a dream, something that stands out from the flow of daily events and speaks to you. It is meant for you alone. You do not want to believe it, you think it is just your imagination, mere fantasy. But it comes again.

Annika had sold her unruly Arabian horse and was looking out for a quiet Haflinger, better suited to her abilities. For a long time she searched in vain and eventually gave up all together the thought of owning a horse. Out walking, a vision came to her from nowhere. Before her inner eye she saw a white Arabian mare complete with details of her age and size: a five-year-old mare, started, measuring some 1.50 m. She saw the horse's head clearly before her. Two more years passed. Till one day she entered a stable and saw the horse from her vision standing in a stall. She inquired about its age: five years old, they had just started training her and she was up for sale. Annika asked the owner the horse's size. He

36

got a rule: 1.50 m. The owner became her husband and today Annika breeds Arabian horses.

The call to adventure is often accompanied by synchronicity, coincidences which are more than coincidence.

Irini had been fired from her job and furthermore had been personally disappointed by the head of the firm. Her search for new work proved to be hopeless. In a moment of great despair she saw a car in front of her with a sticker saying: GO, GO. The car turned into a road called *Jakobstrasse*, James Street. She remembered that she had always wanted to go on a pilgrimage along Saint James' Way, the Camino de Santiago trail. She set off with little money and just a sleeping-bag. She experienced high points and low points, far exceeding those of unemployment, and eventually she learned to trust that life carries you, no matter what comes.

It can happen that the call finds you prepared and waiting to receive a sign, higher permission. It is also possible, that the call reaches you at a time when it does not fit into your life at all.

Vera fell in love with Sundance, a mustang who lived on a ranch in the U.S.A. At the same time her career in a Swiss bank developed in such a way that she was in a financial position to afford the horse's transport across the Atlantic as well as its upkeep in Switzerland.

The only snag was that she was so involved in her new job that she would have little time to take care of the horse. She knew that a mustang, used to endless pastures and life in a herd, could not simply be put in a stable near Zurich, where she would just look in at weekends. But she could not get Sundance off her mind. She dreamt of him and every spare moment she thought about how she could arrange to integrate him into her life. Her obsession led to her withdrawing almost completely from her circle of friends and becoming a loner. Until she decided to go for it.

The owner sold Sundance to her for 2000 dollars, she found a firm to organize the flight to Europe.

At last her dream was to come true. Then the news came that Sundance had died of colic shortly after landing in Amsterdam. The shock was so deep that Vera could hardly drag herself to work. She felt guilty about the horse's death. The whole idea of bringing a mustang to Europe had come to seem completely insane. She simply could not understand how she could let herself be caught up in such an idea.

"I loved him like no other creature in my life before," she told me. I asked her about her first meeting with Sundance.

"I was sitting under a poplar tree out on the prairie, completely still and withdrawn when suddenly I had an intuition to turn round. There was a horse standing behind me, looking at me. No one had ever looked at me that way before, as if he could read me, right into the furthest corner of my soul. He understood me perfectly."

Half a year later Vera gave up her job at the bank and lived on her savings for a while. She wanted to reassess her bearings. It was most moving to watch how her relationship with Sundance continued to affect her beyond his death.

"He is leading me step by step into a new life." She started training as an art therapist and is still working in that profession now. She frequently spends her holidays on the ranch and visits the place where she met Sundance. Till this day she has still not bought a horse of her own. "I already have a horse," she says and smiles.

The call to adventure contains the seed of a story which unfolds in your life if you follow it. Even if it does not always lead you to happiness, it leads you to the truth about yourself.

"Sundance," Vera says today, "represents my longing for freedom and true connection, and I find that in my new profession. I am infinitely grateful to that horse. Because I don't suppose I would have found the way on my own."

The call to adventure contains a profound need of our soul, which at the moment the call reaches us is often unconscious. The only things we perceive are urgency, tension, longing, and they do not fade. We have to follow that need. Everything else withdraws into the background, loses its attraction.

Sometimes the call comes in stages. First very quietly, then louder and louder. It can become so urgent that you cannot breathe if you do not follow it. It is a physical pain, which only disappears when you surrender. The call brings you back into your body, back to your real life.

The Bible and the legends of the saints are full of such calls. Saint Francis of Assisi, from a wealthy merchant family, dreamt of becoming a knight. He was cultured and found himself at the centre of his society. Nevertheless his experiences in war upset him deeply and, on his way to a new battle, he gave his noble clothes to a beggar, fell out with his father and from then on led a life of solitude and poverty, by which he inspired many.

The young Buddha's call reached him when he left his palace for the first time and saw the misery in the streets. He never again went back to his palace and found the way to enlightenment which transcends all suffering.

I give you these dramatic examples to clarify the idea of the call.

In the life of every human being there are such moments which point in a new direction.

I am sure you know such moments, events, developments in your life. Take some time to find such moments in your biography. If you find two or three, write them down. When did the call come? Where from? From whom? What exactly happened? What did you feel? Was it a painful or joyous experience?

Ask yourself what has become of the call. How it has developed? What meaning has been revealed through these developments. By doing this perhaps for the first time in your life, you will become conscious of some of your motives.

Is there a call which is linked to horses? Was it horses that called you? Did an individual horse discover you and awaken you?

Are you able to observe the call to adventure in other people's lives? Even in films and novels? This call is present in most films. In the film *Pretty Woman*, for example, it is the moment when the prostitute Vivian gets into rich man Edward Luis's car to show him the way to Beverly Hills. An apparently insignificant event which changes her life.

The call to adventure can also reach you in the form of a book, as happened to me when I stumbled upon Linda Kohanov's *Tao of Equus* in the New York bookstore *The Strand*. For me the book was, as for many other people, the opening of a new dimension in my dealings with horses and ultimately turned my view of the world upside down. It has brought me to where I am today.

I shall now make a decisive cut to a kind of adventure call which reached me last week as an example of a call that can lead one into very deep waters in the psyche.

In the last few weeks my body has formed an alliance with death. Death is calling me in the form of a seductive young man, who takes me by the hand and wants to lead me into his realm. I wake up, drenched with sweat because I do not want to see what awaits me there.

But when I close my eyes, alluring Death stands before me again and when I go into deep meditation, he is waiting for me there, too. I do not want to go with him because I am afraid that if I take the next step with him, I will die. I first had this dream six months ago. Death all around me. I only have to lift the telephone receiver or open my e-mail box and I receive news from somebody whose mother, son, or horse has died.

Last week, during my stay in the Epona Center in Arizona, Linda Kohanov's stallion Midnight Merlin, one of the most important horses of her career, died. His death, although distressing, was effused with a transcendent meaning which granted all those involved a glimpse of another world. Merlin was a difficult horse but the visionary side of him out-balanced all the difficulties. In one vision he revealed himself to his owner as the reincarnation of a war horse, which was killed by a lance in the chest and whose head had been cut off to rob him off his strength. Linda took him as what he was: a great teacher. He died at the age of 23, just as Linda had seen years before in a vision: not killed by a lance, but by a metal fence post, the only such post on a ranch otherwise fenced with wood.

There is a drawing of Merlin standing head to head with his son

Spirit. It belongs to Linda Kohanov's book *Way of the Horse*, a book with a card set. The card is called like the horse: Midnight Merlin. The morning of Merlin's funeral I was sitting by an enclosure and when I looked up, I saw two real black horses opposite each other just like on Merlin's card. By their posture, which so perfectly embodied Merlin's spirit, the two horses conveyed a message to me about the essence of death. Death is not the end, it is a transition. I would not have understood the message if the horses had not been standing opposite one another that very morning, as if to hold it before me, and if my awareness of such messages from horses had not already been trained. Horses speak to us very quietly and we have to look, listen and feel exactly in order to understand them. Once we have learnt their language, once we have grasped that they speak to us, we understand them easily and wonder why we had so far overlooked the obvious.

My story of Death still goes on. A few weeks later a vicious massacre occurred only a few miles from where I live: a 17-year-old youth killed sixteen people, by shooting most of them in the head, and finally killing himself in the same way.

The night after that I dreamt that my cat laid the torn-off head of our tom-cat at my feet.

Death had finally come very close to me. The next few days I felt as if I was disintegrating like an onion, peeled away layer by layer. It was a frightening process, which triggered in me the feeling that there was nothing left of what I once was.

My old ego had died. Panic-stricken I called Lynne, a meditation teacher who had co-trained our workshop in Arizona, and asked her advice.

"You are in the middle of a transformation process," she said.

"What shall I do?" I wanted to know.

"Trust the process," she replied. "Allow it to carry you."

I now understood the meaning of my death dreams, what Death's invitation to follow him had meant. An old part of myself was to die.

The death of one's old self is part of the birth of the new. It is the story that the hero's journey tells. I was astonished when I saw how this process had crept unnoticed into my own life. And how the stallion Merlin and my cats had played a role in it.

When I had calmed down, I decided to follow Death into his realm by meditating. The realm of Death was a blossoming garden, and in the midst of nature's fullness I found a girl with a horse, with Hadban Enzahi, the proud Arabian stallion. I managed to bring back into my life that lost part of me which could wish and dream innocently. Death became a life-giving elixir for me.

Animals are able to connect us with the world of the invisible and the spiritual. Their symbolic power helps us to go beyond our normal waking state.

"We only have to realize that all the visions and images we experience in nature or in our inner consciousness are valid," writes Ted Andrews in his book *Animal-Speak: The Spiritual & Magical Powers of Creatures Great & Small*. If we observe nature attentively, it becomes an open book. Then we recognize the call to adventure everywhere, the call to undertake a journey and to find once more that world which our ancestors knew so well and whose only messengers left today appear to be animals. Man is some 5 million years old and for 4,999 million years nature has been his teacher.

"It will be animals," says my friend Andrea, "who will bring us out of the misery we are trapped in. If *they* don't do it, then there is nobody, and we are lost." We have lost so much of our instinctive knowledge, so much of the consciousness that shows us how we can survive, that we walk through the world like the blind and do not recognize the solution, even if it lies at our feet.

That is why it is so important for us to follow the call when it rings out. If we do that honestly, it will lead us back into the heart of the creature and will connect us to a power far greater than us, to the rhythm and energy of the cosmos.

Many women, who had known Merlin and had learnt from him, came to his funeral from all directions. They stood in a circle around his grave, piled up with stones on the ranch, and told stories about him. These were intelligent and wise stories told by intelligent and wise women. And for a short while around the grave there arose the tenderness of the matriarchy, which embraces life and death, which belong together.

As I was departing from the ranch the next day, I took photos of Merlin's grave and I saw under fleecy clouds part of a rainbow sparkling in the blue sky.

If you own an animal or have contact with one, find time to do some activities with it. You can also walk in nature and listen to birds or observe cows, horses, sheep or goats in the pasture. The most important thing is that you completely focus on the animal, that you fine-tune your perception and that you learn to understand the messages of movements, sounds and gestures, and eventually also perceive the intuitive images that they activate inside you.

44

If you listen closely to an animal, you will find out that it has a message for you. Perhaps you have long been waiting for a call, maybe you feel tired, exhausted, or you are curious and impatient. The call is within you, it is waiting to be heard. Go and ask the animals. Then follow them.

Step Three
The Wound

The call to adventure comes in various forms. But when a horse is involved, vulnerability is always a factor. In her books Linda Kohanov has confronted that difference between fear and vulnerability which is so important for people who handle horses. And not only for horse people, for all creative people. And therefore for every living creature on this planet. Fear is a reaction to an external threat which makes us seek security. Vulnerability is a reaction to an internal threat. When we are really creative, we expose ourselves to the unknown, to the unpredictable. We bring great strength into our lives with this exposure, for we tune in to the magic of creation, but we also leave behind the old security and order in which we felt protected. That arouses a barely manageable fear which has no external causes.

The call to adventure has catapulted us out of our habits. Suddenly there is a horse in our lives. It is large, it is dangerous, its nature is unknown. We approach it, it retreats, we ask it to do something, it resists. It stops or runs off, it bucks, it shies, it bites, it kicks, it drags us through the riding arena on our lead rope.

Few people, who fulfill their wish for a horse of their own, suspect that a horse not only costs time and money, it also turns their sense of emotional security upside down. Few suspect that the horse will transform them into different people.

In the life of every horse-person the moment comes when the horse inflicts a wound on them, a physical or an emotional wound.

The third step of the hero's journey deals with the wound we bear within us and which horses find with unfailing intuition.

We have followed the call but what awaits us is no Sunday walk. Only now is the journey really beginning. The magic of the beginning has evaporated. The reality of our new world receives us. The horse is in the stable and produces manure. It is hungry and has special feeding needs. It is not enough simply to throw it a pile of hay every day. Horses' stomachs want to be busy round the clock. The horse demands exercise even when it is raining cats and dogs. The new saddle pinches, the bridle does not fit. The horse develops whims and quirks faster than you can imagine.

With our usual strategies we can compensate for much of this but then the moment comes when the horse reveals the wound. It finds our blind spot, that shadow we refuse to recognize.

That feeling of vulnerability which we try to hide when we confidently enter the stable. They see right through our performance.

Stefanie, a young woman with an impressively self-confident appearance, bubbling with humour and witty remarks, fell in love with the gelding Timberland, a strong, young cross breed, the very horse she had always wanted, young and mouldable.

Many horse enthusiasts buy unstarted horses, partly because they are free to train them according to their preconceptions but also because they can afford them. In this way inexperienced horse owners come up against inexperienced horses. To begin with the relationship between Stefanie and Timberland developed positively. Every day after work Stefanie appeared in the stable, cleaned and groomed her horse until the hooves gleamed.

She went on walks with Timberland and in the beginning he cooperated. It is to the credit of the Natural Horsemanship movement that young horses are trained on the ground with great patience. That means they learn to give in to pressure, allow themselves to be touched and to react to fine signals, before a rider lowers himself onto their backs like a predator ready to inflict the fatal bite. This is how the horse gains self-confidence and trust in human beings.

Stefanie, however, belongs to that sort of rider who cannot wait to get onto the horse and ride off into the sunset. At this point I would like to state that I myself was by no means any better. Although I knew ground work, I preferred to see myself as a cowgirl, sweeping off on an Arabian bird. What saved me from Stefanie's fate was perhaps just luck.

A few weeks later I saw Stefanie out for a walk with Timberland and it took my breath away. The horse was so tense that I was afraid it would explode any minute. His head was stretched upwards, his eyes wide open, his flanks quivering. Young horses are unpredictable. A rustling in the bushes can cause them to hurtle off in a fraction of a second and, with their youthful lack of coordination, they drag the person leading them along behind.

I asked Stephanie if everything was okay. She laughed cheerfully and said: "He is just a bit high-spirited. He'll settle down." The fact that Stefanie did not seem to realize the danger worried me even more than the horse. Quite the opposite, she was proud of her courage. My heart sank. I felt obliged to express my concern.

"Don't you think it would be better to exercise Timberland in an enclosed space first?"

"Look to your own horse. It's not that calm either," Stefanie's look could have laid out an elephant. I understood that her self-confidence was just a thin protective layer. No way was she the tough Amazon she wished to appear as. That is not the point anyway when handling horses, even if many people think that.

Horses feel our fear. There is no place in our bodies, in our feelings, in our thoughts, in our consciousness where we can hide our fear from them. A horse's perception is far more sensitive than most people can imagine.

Stefanie had no control over her horse because he did not trust her. Timberland repeatedly received contradictory signals from her. We know that from human behaviour. Somebody acts strong and we know full well that it is not genuine. While Stefanie presented herself as especially carefree, Timberland felt the fear and insecurity expressed through her bodily tension. The young horse felt abandoned by his leader and reacted by panicking.

Horses need a leader who is centered, whose body is not separated from his head. The split of head and body, however, is the norm in our civilization. We have not learnt to be at one with our body or our feelings. We live primarily in our heads.

In our thoughts we wander hither and thither and only rarely do we connect with the present moment, the place where horses are at home. Horses live in the pure present, and they find a head without a body very frightening.

Stefanie bought an expensive saddle, riding boots, bridle and crop. One day I walked into the stable to see an ambulance at the gate. Stefanie had gone out riding for the first time and Timberland had bucked her off. One of his hooves had struck her chest, the other had hit the ground a mere hand's breadth from her face. She could have been dead.

I have a friend who always falls in love with men who hurt her, sometimes even hit her. To her mind these men are especially sensitive and need a lot of understanding. She does not understand why men suddenly react aggressively. She does not recognize the signs. I wanted to take my friend with me to my mare, so that she could feel in every fibre of her body when danger threatened. But she is afraid of horses. With patience I eventually managed to persuade her to exchange her high heels for Wellingtons.

"Imagine the horse is Thomas," I said, deliberately using the name of her latest conquest. She was shaking and trembling as she approached my well-behaved mare. She did not want to believe that the horse could have anything to do with her love affairs.

The amazing thing was that Tinnia snuggled up to Silke with a tenderness she rarely shows. Silke's resistance melted away like glacial ice in spring. From one moment to the next the frightening horse was the favourite of favourites. She hugged and caressed the mare as if she wanted to drown her in feelings.

"She understands me to the very depths of my soul," Silke enthused. "Such a darling horse."

Whoosh, the mare pinned back her ears and her muzzle shot forward with bared teeth, hardly missing the sleeve of Silke's blouse. Silke jumped back shocked. Her body froze, her eyes were vacant. Her mind had fled to some distant hide-away.

"Everything alright, Silke?"

Then, suddenly, as if somebody had flicked a switch, she returned and smiled. "I just don't know anything about horses."

"Everything alright?" I asked again.

"Of course—what d'you mean?"

I did not believe her—and she noticed.

"To be honest I could burst out crying," she said as her cheerful expression collapsed. "The horse behaves just as badly as Thomas. First he is really nice and then suddenly he attacks me. I just don't understand it. What did I do wrong?"

She wanted to go home but instead decided to stay and sit down with me on a bale of straw at a safe distance.

"You thought the horse was really nice and then you were surprised by the opposite."

"It is funny, but when I said the horse was really nice, I felt that it wasn't true. It felt false, exaggerated, as if I was only acting out the feeling, not really experiencing it."

"What did you really feel?"

"I was moved that the horse snuggled up to me, but when I started to hug it, I noticed that it withdrew. Instead of stopping, however, I carried on because I could not bear being rejected. And then all the falseness began."

"Did it reject you then?"

"Not exactly. I felt it withdraw and only when I continued to pressure it, did it resist." She was silent for a while. "I should have stopped when I noticed that the horse had had enough." She went silent again. "But if I do that, I never get the love I need. I am probably condemned to eternal loneliness because not even a huge animal like a horse can accept my feelings." Silke became very silent and sad.

As Silke was transformed into a picture of misery, my mare came towards us. She laid her muzzle on Silke's shoulder and for a long time stood with her in complete silence. Suddenly I heard sobbing. Silke just sat there, there was no exuberant declaration of love, instead there was an endlessly extended moment of closeness.

The call to adventure always has two sides: a light and a dark one. My vision of Hadban Enzahi, the Arabian breeding stallion, was as bright as the light issuing from the Indian myth about the origin of the horse: "From the sun, ye shining gods, you have made a horse!"

No matter how bright the vision may be, there comes a moment when the first cracks begin to show. Cracks through which darkness, danger and injury leak out. The hero's journey is a descent into the shadow world, into the realm of suppressed feelings. The sooner you perceive the darkness, the better you will be armed. Then you will see danger lurking before it kicks you in the chest in the form of the horse's hoof. Then instead of being a source of danger, horses become healers, as in Silke's story.

"What I considered to be love, that insatiable feeling," Silke told me later, "was not love at all. Love is what I felt when I was completely silent. The longing for more and more had disappeared because I had found what I had always been looking for. I still can't believe that it was a horse that gave me that insight."

Shortly after that she broke up with Thomas and I noticed that none of the usual candidates muscled into her life either. When I asked her about it, she confided in me the following: "That afternoon I promised Tinnia that I would never again get involved with something other than what she had shown me. Since then I feel so much better—and to be honest, I'm in no hurry at all."

Why do we get involved in journeys, which lead us into darkness? Why did Stefanie not sell her horse after her bad accident, but keep it? Often the journey only begins with the accident. That appears to be the message which many people find in the depths of pain, like sunken treasure. To separate from the horse would mean rejecting the call to adventure. It would mean breaking off the journey shortly after starting it. Something in the human soul appears to resist that as if survival depended on it. And survival is what it is all about. The soul longs for the journey. The journey is its only goal. With the journey it fulfills its life purpose.

On the journey the darkness of the accident transforms itself into something different. If you do not treat the accident as coincidence but as a call in the highest sense, it becomes a tragic occurence. The purpose of tragedy is catharsis, purification. This at least is what the Greek philosopher Aristotle teaches us with our civilization's first theory of tragedy.

A tragic occurrence points out beyond our one-dimensional perception of reality. The relevance of tragedy is transcendence, transgression. Tragedy connects us to a transcendent world, which turns the meaning of an event into its opposite. Something fatal becomes something vital. Pain becomes a way towards the light.

For people with our cultural background this is difficult to understand. We have lost the meaning of tragedy. For us there is negative and positive, either the one or the other. An accident is negative, we want to forget it as soon as possible.

Horses teach us something different. Horses teach us that dark is light and light is dark. They do not judge, they dance. The dance of darkness which is transformed into light.

Stefanie has begun to work with her horse, not with the stylish saddle or the hoof polish. Every day she takes her gelding into the round pen and tries to communicate with him, studies his reactions, his movements, his snorting and chewing, the swish of his tail. She feels when he is anxious and when he is calm. Recently I saw him weaving along beside her without a bridle. That kind of thing does not happen unless the person changes as well. Silke is still cheerful, but her self-confidence is now genuine. Because she has come to know herself. You cannot get to know a horse's body without being aware of your own. Because communication with a horse goes via the body—or it does not go at all.

In his book *The Soul of Screenwriting*, the most impressive book I know on the hero's journey, Keith Cunningham presents the Greek myth of Actaeon, the hunter, as an example of the essence of tragedy. Actaeon, an ambitious hero who hitherto succeeded in everything, is searching for worthy prey. He discovers the goddess Artemis and her nymphs bathing. Nobody has ever seen the virgin goddess naked before. The goddess is furious and splashes water into his face: "Go and tell everybody that you have seen the naked goddess–if you can." But before Actaeon can flee, she transforms him into a deer and his hunting dogs tear him to pieces.

Our contemporary reaction would be a feeling of satisfaction that he received his just deserts. But the myth celebrates Actaeon's death as fulfillment. Actaeon had found his true prey: the sight of the goddess causes the death of his earthly ego. The gate to transcendence opened for him. In death the hero completed his journey.

"The purpose of tragedy," Cunningham writes, "is to say yes to the circumstances which life brings." Actaeon has fulfilled his life purpose. He has reached the source and has recognized his deepest nature.

Horses connect us to an archaic view of things. For horses there is no such thing as good or bad. For horses there is only being in the moment, which is always perfect. Outside of that there is no life, no creativity, there are only illusions in the mind.

The presence of horses liberates us from such illusions. They bounce off horses and dissolve into thin air. To be free of them fills one with joy and renewal.

Behind the illusions our true feelings show themselves, like true love for Silke and true self-confidence for Stefanie. Stefanie's accident was painful, two broken ribs, a broken forearm. With one kick the horse had shattered her false self. What remained was not only a damaged body, but a self from which all the air had been let out. For days on end she did not dare to look anybody in the eye, because she felt she was a failure. In our culture defeat represents a terminus, disgrace, exposure. We are naked, our masks have been removed. The hunter Actaeon meets his dream image, but before he can carry his triumph back to his tribe, his vainglorious ego is torn to shreds.

Where we give up, feel like failures, that is the starting point for horses. At last we are normal. At last we have awoken from our illusionary dreams.

Nowadays every step I take off the way, when I submit to self-righteousness, is accompanied by such great pain, that I can hardly bear it. Waves of fear sweep over me and my vulnerability is as raw as that of a baby abandoned on an ice-cold winter night.

And then there are moments when the veil is torn open and I recognize what is actually hidden behind it: a longing to find my Self, which has been suppressed for too long, which I can no longer hold in check, which presses forward like a leading mare in search of the water which will save her herd. And the mare gallops off, nothing can hold her back.

Our life is full of wounds. We could draw up long lists. Or we forget about lists and count the wonderful moments of happiness. I belong to the cheerful kind of people who like to see life as a game. Whether we torment ourselves with depression or play the clown makes no difference to horses. They look right through us. We only have to move close to them to receive our lesson. Sooner or later a horse will find our one weak spot, the hook on which we have hung our ego. In an unguarded moment and with impressive accuracy they tear the ego free of its anchorage.

The blurb to Timo Ameruoso's book: *Zweierlei Leben − Mein schmerzhafter Weg zu wahrer Erkenntnis* (Two Different Lives–My Painful Way to True Knowledge) refers to this: "At the height of my boisterousness and arrogance, a success at show-jumping, life dealt me a fateful blow … Looking back to my active time, I would describe myself as a rider just like all the others. I never really understood my horse ... The most difficult thing about working with a horse is working on oneself." I have been spared the fate of Timo Ameruoso. After a fall he was confined to a wheelchair. Horses have dealt out their lessons to me in smaller doses. And I consider myself lucky that those lessons have affected me so deeply that I have not needed more severe blows.

An apparently small event thus became a lesson for me, which I remember again and again because it is of such great importance for my Being, for my life path.

Once I had understood the basics of Natural Horsemanship, I considered myself capable of training an unhandled, four-year-old horse. The owner of the farm where I kept my mare offered to let me start Scarlotta for later use as a second riding horse for my daughter. I enjoy adventure, and when I hear that starting a young horse is the most difficult of all tasks, my ambition is aroused. Ambition, that quality, which–like vanity–you should leave at home when handling horses.

I read the relevant books and attended Birger Gieseke's *Horseman Rendezvous*, which focused on training young horses. There I was able to watch a number of very gifted trainers like Honza Blaha, Silke Valentin, Johannes Beck Broichsitter and Bernd Hackl working with young horses. To start with I made good progress with Scarlotta. She was intelligent and learnt quickly. Too quickly. One day she managed to yank the rope out of my hand. She had won the game, and did so again the next day. I was determined to stick with it, but my knees were knocking by the time I had finished my training units. It was too much for me but I was not yet prepared to admit to my incompetence. One fine day I was lungeing Scarlotta in the round pen under the guidance of my riding teacher, Astrid, whom I had called in for advice. I managed a few good circuits. I was contented—and proud. I blurted out my pride to everybody.

"Just look at how well the horse is moving." I had hardly uttered my sentence when Scarlotta started to buck. The rope tightened and my little finger got trapped. It was only my little finger. And after several weeks of numbness it was alright again. But since then I really leave vanity out of it when I enter the arena with a horse. For a brief moment my vanity had distracted me from the situation. Scarlotta took advantage of this moment to give vent to her high spirits. I think of this experience whenever I notice my pride rising. Vanity and pride are two quite useless qualities, they catapult me out of the present moment, dilute my attention and just produce shallow satisfaction. I can do without that.

Thanks to Scarlotta I understood what the Buddhists mean by 'non attachment': perceiving feelings when they arise but without submitting to them, letting them go immediately. Had I mastered this art earlier, things would have gone differently with Scarlotta.

A horse, especially a young one, notices even your slightest inattention. It loses confidence in you as its leader. Horses need a person who is present. Being actually there is the best thing we can do for them. In every individual moment. I finally gave up training Scarlotta because I was not up to her watchfulness. It was too dangerous. She was too big, too strong, too fast for me.

Watchfulness, attention have remained paramount for me. In relationships, in my creative work. If I am not attentive, the text vanishes from my head before I can write it down.

The ability of an author, of every artist, of every human being depends on how attentive he is, how long he can maintain concentration without escaping.

Life is an art of attentiveness.

Attention involves not evading unpleasant perceptions. It is not easy to live in the present. Our small and large evasions are established habits. To flee from a situation is a basic reflex in our culture, a culture of flight. To give just a trivial example: our work becomes boring—we reach for the chocolate supply. Suddenly half the bar is gone. Where were we?

Will horses become our trainers? To put it another way: can a human trainer dole out such effective lessons as a four-year-old mare can? In recent years a method has been developed which employs horses for training people in leadership. Just as character was once trained by using horses, nowadays people in responsible positions, who have never seen a horse before, are sent into the ring with a horse. Can horses lead us out of the economic crisis? Just like in earlier times when they facilitated military successes, not on the battlefield now, however, but in the round pen?

I wanted to talk about wounds.

You do not acquire attentiveness by trying hard to concentrate. Being attentive means exposing yourself to pain. We are so trained to flee into happiness and pleasure that we do not grasp our inability to live until a horse traps our little finger, treads on our foot or breaks our ribs. A simple exercise points up the whole dilemma: lead your horse past a rich green pasture without it lowering its head to graze.

My friend Heike, a Qi Gong teacher who has been meditating for years, produced an impressive example of attentiveness. She was very frightened of horses until I suggested she go into the pasture to meditate with Tinnia. Juicy, knee-high spring grass swayed round Tinnia's slim fetlocks, yet she stood there motionless with

Heike for a full twenty minutes. Heike had something to offer her that she found more tempting than the sweet swishing grass. An impressive example of the role consciousness plays when handling horses.

When the wound splits open, a battle begins. Our need to flee becomes as overwhelming as the alcoholic's need for a slug of whisky. We get caught in a terrible test of nerves. We have no wish to see what is bleeding within us, yet at the same time we know there is no way back. For we have seen.

What is my wound? Insufficient appreciation. Although I work hard I have difficultly acknowledging my own achievements. I am addicted to other people's recognition and approval. I need such statements as: "You're great, you're exceptional…" just as the alcoholic craves the bottle. When approval is absent for a while, when criticism and failures pile up, I start becoming uneasy, then panicky, and finally I lose my head. Is my wound the fear of being insufficiently loved? I frequently recognize this fear amongst horse people. With bags full of carrots they spend every free moment with those big-hearted animals who appear to absorb all the pain like giant garbage chutes.

Frequently I think of the philosopher Friedrich Nietzsche, who, so the story goes, clasped a poor coach horse round the neck because he saw in him a fellow sufferer. How deeply he must have felt the creature's suffering and seen it as a reflection of his own. A breakthrough in insight which was extremely rare amongst his contemporaries, and all reports of this event portray Nietzsche as mentally deranged, as if such a testimony of feeling was otherwise unthinkable.

I have often flung my arms round my mare's neck weeping and

I am sure I am not the only one.

Let us go deeper into the wound. What is your wound? Do you have the courage to express it out loud? You have submitted to a process which is now running its course and you are right in the middle of it. Every morning you wake up with new pain. Sometimes you succeed in healing it. If not, it is waiting for you the very next morning. If you have healed it, new pain awaits you. Take time to go into it...

I have no idea when my pain will come to rest. I only know that I am right in the middle of it and have been for some time. My sensors are so wide open that I only need to snap fingers to intuitively receive highly relevant information. My mare Tinnia is my channel. I concentrate on her and she sends me the data. I need her in order to be certain that the information does not come from within me but from the morphic field, the collective unconscious or whatever it may be called.

These days I wake up with a stabbing pain in my stomach which spurs me on to constantly new self study. Once I have found the answer the pain vanishes. Pain is, like horses, a great teacher.

Today I succeeded in dissolving the pain only to reveal a deeper pain beneath it. While I am helplessly exposed to this weakness, my old ego is burnt up and my perception becomes so subtle that I move a little closer to the horse's perception which is so many light-years subtler than ours. Our unresolved pain keeps us from seeing clearly, from seeing brightly. Horses feel that. They only open themselves completely to people who know their own wounds. To them a person who does not know himself is unpredictable, untrustworthy as a leader, in some circumstances life-threatening. He cannot protect them from the predator.

In her greatest pain after losing her husband, Carol went to the coral in the dark in order to find solace with the horses. One of the animals approached her, laid its head on her shoulder and blew breath into her ear. She stood with him for a long time, feeling his warmth. One of the co-workers on the Apache Springs Ranch discovered Carol and told her to get away from the horse as fast as she could. It was Merlin, the stallion who usually never let anyone near him. Who was notorious for abruptly attacking people. In our pain the only choice is to be authentic. Carol's authenticity aroused Merlin's trust.

After I understood that this is where everything begins, that authenticity is the most fundamental characteristic we need for horses to accept us as partners, many things in my life changed. The world I live in seems to me even more insane than before, a dance of lost souls, cut off from all genuine experience.

Pain, the wound, is the bridge to Being. Pain is there to give us information about our cure. To feel it means letting fresh water flow into a polluted pool. Endure this pain. Then I can continue my life on a new basis. Then I can come closer to my horse. Then my writing can become more authentic, my relationships more human.

Pain transforms itself into fear. What am I afraid of? The answer is not fear, it is vulnerability. This one vital feeling that is so characteristic of every form of creativity, characteristic of the gentleness, we need to do justice to the infinite gentleness of horses.

The message behind vulnerability is that we are just as shy as horses, that we long for genuine encounters. I remember that as a girl I searched for true being behind false appearances, that condition which resembles the setting sun after an overheated summer day. I remember that that is why I am with horses. Because I will always find it there.

It was horses who early in my life gave me access to this realm, who saved me from freezing solid, rescued me from living decay.

I suddenly feel very sad. Because I have become aware how often I have left this realm, have forgotten the horses and all the unspoiled beauty that accompanies them. Then I calm down and the tension slackens.

I think of my friend Andrea, who wrote to me that intuitive people are not noticed because their power is invisible to others and that is why she feels excluded and unnoticed. I want to tell Andrea that I see her, that horses see us and that many people see us. That many people will find the key, just as I have found it. Am I not here writing this book? In my other books I do not see myself. It is a strange feeling to see myself–me!

This is where my cure lies. Seeing myself. Not my ego. Not my mask. Not my outward appearance, but my essence. The light.

What my horse sees.

Can I stay with myself and not flee? That is my task. That is the mother's milk I long for. I myself am the milk. I am the one who prepares it. I am the provider and the nourishment.

I see myself–that is all. That is enough.

I can feed others and myself. Others feed me and I feed them.

That is the message. The pain, the vulnerability have disappeared and my body fills with warmth, with well-being, my breath smells as sweet as a freshly plucked apple.

I have found the answer.

Now I can begin the day and find solutions for the tangible tasks. The house, its management.

I give thanks to Tinnia. Afterwards I shall go with her to the arena and play. She has just told me: that is her wish.

The hero's journey is such a wonderful model because it provides a frame for seemingly disconnected and insignificant events. No matter whether it is a fictional story or one's own life, whether it is a psychological or a spiritual journey. Events are brought together through the hero's journey, it uncovers their meaning. When the hero's journey is at stake, suddenly a story is revealed. Horses are catalysts for the hero's journey. They thrust us towards our wounds and they understand how to heal them.

Now it is up to you to give your wound a name. Proceed carefully and do not give in to deception. Your wound is the gateway to the depths of the hero's journey. It is the key to the heart of the creature. Ask your horse, ask the sunrise. Do not accept the slightest whiff of falsehood. Weep, bid your tears welcome. Be gentle with your fear. Select your words with care as they flow from your soul. Take this step and do not look back. What is your story? What wounds have horses inflicted on you? Have you enquired about the messages beneath your wounds? Did you stand up again to walk on? And where did your path lead you?

You understand that an honest answer is required. That

there is no other answer. That here you will perhaps experience not happiness but healing. Can you walk through the storm until you find the new truth?

Can you see yourself? The clear picture–now that you are a human being who has not only strengths and weaknesses but also wounds.

If you wish make a drawing.

Have you felt the moment when the horse bowed to you and said: Now you are here. Welcome to my world!

Step Four
The Goal

Where horses are concerned goals are often involved. The horse is expected to jump over some hurdle, is expected to run with the correct (even) gait. There are specific terms for each goal. The training range of the Riding Association, the levels in Natural Horsemanship, the dressage classifications. Catching your horse out in the pasture or lifting its hoof can also constitute a goal.

With all these goals the horse is expected to do what the human being demands of it. Why should it? It was born to graze on the steppes. Nothing else.

Let us consider the hero's journey of horses. What goals do they pursue? Why are they still here even though we no longer need them and when they do not fit into modern civilization at all?

I did my first workshop in so-called equine-facilitated learning in

Ireland on Yvonne Monahan's farm by the sea on fairy-tale land where horses graze under ancient, ivy-clad trees where fairies dwell. That is where I met Cisco, a black and white paint horse. He awakened my sense of smell. Suddenly I was able to perceive the unknown smells of cinnamon-dusted brimstone butterflies and toads tangled in seaweed - smells I did not know existed. When the horses in the adjacent paddocks noticed how grateful and happy I felt about that, they hurried over to join Cisco to reveal even more secrets. Unfortunately the exercise was then already over. But the day had only just began. In the afternoon Cisco and I shared the honour of meeting in the round pen.

At that time I was still a novice in spiritual things, just curious and, as a writer, in search of interesting material. Before I entered the ring with Cisco, Yvonne Monahan asked me to formulate my heart's desire. I turned to Cisco and said, "take me with you on a spiritual journey". It seemed to me to be the most interesting thing I could imagine at that point in time. I wanted to know.

What happened then was nothing spectacular, for outsiders it may have been nothing more than a woman moving around a horse. But for me it was an initial experience, a further initiation into the secret power of horses.

The perception of one's own body is central in this approach developed by Linda Kohanov. Before I entered the ring, I was asked to name a part of my body which was in pain or under stress. I chose my left shoulder. In the round pen with Cisco I had no idea where to start. Unlike when I do free longeing or ground work with my mare, I had no specific goal. And no idea whatsoever what a spiritual journey with a horse should look like.

Cisco and I hung around in the round pen for a while, he was noticeably restless. Again and again he ran past me. Each time I turned he again ran past me. I was afraid that this was all nonsense and would not produce any kind of result. Either the method was garbage or I was too insensitive or incapable.

Because I normally tend to expect quick results I was gradually becoming desperate. Then I realized there was method in Cisco's apparently aimless wanderings. He was trying somehow to get on my left side while I, without being aware of it, forced him back to my right, simply to be somehow in control. I had learned that the human being was the horse's boss.

When I finally allowed him to move to my left, he stopped, chewed and licked extensively. He was contented. I too felt calmer, my doubts and my insecurity disappeared.

The thought occurred to me that Cisco's position could have something to do with the pain in my left shoulder. I reached out a hand to Cisco's shoulder and touched him. It felt good. He seemed to have wanted precisely that because he lowered his head and sighed. I felt warmth flow through my arm. It was energy coming from Cisco and it blew away the pain in my shoulder like the down from a chick.

The consequences of this experience, as unspectacular as it was, triggered a fundamental change of heart in me. I do not know why but it came as a shock at an existential level. Presumably because I had understood that a horse has some kind of healing conscious-ness. A horse! A horse!!!

Cisco showed me that he possesses healing powers and that meant that he actually had taken me with him on a spiritual jour-ney.

Many people will certainly find this hard to believe. But for me it was an experience from which there was no turning back. It was the first of many experiences which were to follow and which repeatedly confirmed the same thing: horses have consciousness. In some way that changed everything for me: my association with horses, my view of human beings, my philosophy of living and ultimately my whole life. When I stepped into the ring with Cisco, I had set a goal for myself, not the usual man-horse goal. And Cisco took me at my word. Cisco, a horse…

It just comes to me now to open the *Tao Te Ching*, a 2700-year-old book about natural spirituality which also inspired Linda Kohanov. I open it at random … I would like to quote you the passage I have found:

"The simplest exemplar is the clearest.

Contented with a normal life,

you can show all men the Way

back to their own true nature."

Is there a greater philosopher than Cisco?

The first three steps of a hero's journey are a kind of prelude. It really starts properly with the 4th step, the goal. We now know who we are and with this knowledge as support we set off in a specific direction.

It is all a question of direction and decision.

When I brought my mare into my life, it was my intention to

find relaxation by going riding and relying on her as research material for my horse novels. Today I am research material for my horse! She tries to find out what kinds of adventures she can still lead me to. I follow her suggestions. By doing that my life has acquired tremendous dynamism.

What is your goal with horses?

Perhaps this all seems interesting to you but rather high-flown. I can understand that. Perhaps you're thinking: I don't have the ability to handle horses in such a way or even to hear their voices.

I didn't used to have this ability either. I am not a professional rider, nor a professional medium. But anybody who takes the trouble can learn to do what I do with horses within a few years, in their spare time.

If you really tune in to a horse, it will answer you. It's all up to you. Whether you're prepared to throw your prejudices overboard and see horses with different eyes, recognize their tremendous abilities, honoured so long ago in the ancient myths. Anybody can do it. The workshops in equine-facilitated learning are so wonderful because there you experience what abilities not only horses but also humans have.

What is your goal? Write it down now before you read on. It will perhaps change before you have read to the end of the chapter. Then you will be able to return to this moment, to your first impulse. You remember that it's about moments, not about right or wrong, not about good or bad. What is your goal with horses? And with yourself?

Are you a horse owner? Do you share your horse with someone else? Have horses always been special creatures in your life even if you never got particularly close to them? Many people have an intense relationship to this animal even if they have never ridden, live in a city or have no room for horses in their lives. Nonetheless they are close to them in dreams, in thoughts, in their world of feeling. One of the participants in our horse workshops described her love of horses in a questionnaire like this:

"In my childhood enthusiasm a cow had to stand in as a horse because there were no horses when I was a child. My grandparents had a small farm, there I tamed a bull calf which I christened 'Black Beauty'. I had a sack and a rope, they served as saddle and reins. Every evening when Granny took me with her to do the milking, I saddled 'Black Beauty'. Grandpa lifted me onto the 'horse's' back. I was so enthusiastic that even a cow became a horse."

You do not have to own a horse, do not even have to enter a riding stable in order to be close to the spirit of horses. Their spirit is available to everybody. The photograph of my dream stallion Hadban Enzahi accompanied me throughout my youth and inspired me in countless ways. It was just a piece of cardboard. A postcard from a calendar. But every time I looked at the horse it felt like home to me.

What is your relationship to horses? What is their position in your life? What dreams do you have of them?

This step of the hero's journey is about manifestation. Our

dreams solidify to a concrete goal. They enter the process of becoming real. They are supposed to become reality. Without reality they remain the gossamer of dreams. Illusions, in which you imprison the truth about yourself and your journey.

What is reality? A stable full of manure, a lame horse, an exorbitant vet's bill?

The opposite can happen as well: you have too few dreams, too few illusions, your reality has become so inflexible that you have forgotten how to dream. Dreams are part of life, they are the playthings of the mind in search of solutions.

What is a goal? It is a signpost to unknown territory. You do not know whether you will ever get there. Whether you will get stuck, turn round, or will pursue a new goal en route. Whether the goal will turn out to be non-existent as for Christopher Columbus who was looking for the sea route to India.

The goal gives you a direction and it gives you a motive. It gives you the energy of directed movement. A goal gives you the freedom to take the first step.

The reason why you want to reach your goal will influence the way you go. Is your goal Santiago de Compostella and your motive the search for personal spirituality? Your motive will transform an ordinary walk into a pilgrimage.

A goal gives your journey a name. A goal is a contract you make with yourself. Whether you will arrive or not is unimportant just now. What is important is that you set off and that you have a direction.

The English woman Joanne's goal is to find the highest wisdom our civilization can offer. I met Joanne on Linda Kohanov's ranch.

Joanne has already come very close to her goal. A few months ago she was still tied up in a career in public relations in London. My goal was writing horse novels. Now I have a new goal: accompanying people on their hero's journey with horses.

What is your goal? Do you want to be close to horses? Experience their wisdom and integrate it into your life? You are reading this book. Why? What do you expect to gain from it?

The goal will from now on determine the direction of your journey. If you want to make the journey, decide on a goal. Write it down. Phrase it clearly. Reread your spontaneous answer to the question about your goal at the beginning of the chapter. Be simple and decisive in naming your goal. Have the courage to express what you have long known. Have you answered the questions in the previous steps? All that has gone before is part of the preparation for the journey. When you have named your goal, you will cross the border to its realization. You will enter the unknown realm where the treasure awaits you. The horse will lead you there.

The goal need not be a major one. It can be something apparently insignificant like the wish to see a happy, contented expression on your horse's face. If you love challenges, you might want to set yourself a seemingly unattainable major goal like Silke Valentin who although tied to a wheelchair wanted to become a horse trainer. Silke Valentin trains Friesian horses and is an internationally renowned teacher.

I decided to make my goal more concrete. My goal is to complete this book, make my hero's journey an invitation to you to undertake your own heroic journey.

It occurs to me to draw one of the horse cards that Linda Kohanov designed together with the artist Kim McElroy. The forty cards represent a way of initiation, similar to the hero's journey. The meaning of the cards is described in Linda Kohanov's book *Way of The Horse*.

I draw the card with the intention of finding out something about the motif which can help me reach my goal.

I suggest you draw a card as well, perhaps you own oracle cards like the Tarot or open at random a philosophical, spiritual or religious book, the Bible if you wish, the Tao Te Ching, or any other book that resonates for you.

This is an intuitive technique for finding a message. I cut the deck of cards—face down—in two. (You can proceed likewise with a book.) Then I feel which pile the card I am looking for is in. I try to pick up information in the form of energy. When I have selected one pile, I keep repeating the procedure—until I have only two cards left to choose from. (In a book that would be two pages.) Even in spiritual matters precision can give you security.

The card (My cat Mia made the final choice by climbing onto the stool and placing her paw on one of the cards.):

22: Stillness

The wise grey mare watches over her herd with a calm mind and an open heart.

Abilities: Patience and equanimity, keep calm when you are under pressure. A passive style of leadership.

The challenge: The most effective leader gives up the ambition of mastering the way in order to be a master of himself instead.

What message did you get? Write it down.

You now have a goal, whatever it looks like, and you have a message saying which attitude, which motif will help you achieve your goal. I call it a mantra, a spiritual formula which will accompany you in realizing your goal.

I will now ask you to draw up a contract with yourself.

You write down your name, your goal and your motif (mantra), as well as the date.

I, Nina Kolkrabe, hereby draw up a contract with myself for the attainment of the following goal:

(Example) I would like to experience what it really means to be at one with a horse.

My mantra: (example) He who is rigid and stiff is a pupil of death. He who is soft and flexible is a pupil of life. (Tao Te Ching)

Wiesbaden, 23rd March 2012

Your signature

The moment has come for us to cross the border and go out into open country. Goals play an important role in our culture, especially in our work. In businesses agreements and deadlines are made, work is broken down into steps, into processes, into mini-units. We would also like to do this in our work with horses, the purpose of whose existence is to move grazing across the steppes.

We would also like a points system for our soul to be able to measure our achievements. With the way of the spirit it is not a question of achievement but of surrender. And likewise for the way with horses. The spiritual teacher Ram Dass writes, "For us in the West surrender is a word with highly unpleasant connotations, horrible things like the political I-accept-your-capitulation are connected to it, baring your neck to the stronger as a sign of submission and so on."

Surrender is nothing but love. There is no love without surrender. Thinking in terms of achievement and a points system for assessing our progress will not bring us love. Not the love of horses. Nor even the attention they grant us. At the most it will produce resistance. Have we gone amongst horses for that? Is their submission our goal when we see them galloping through our daydreams with their manes streaming behind them?

If reaching our goal is not a question of achievement, how should we then achieve it? Can one reach a goal by surrendering? Does surrender not mean submitting to the stream of life and allowing it to carry us where it will? Do we not lose sight of all goals in doing that? Achievement and surrender seem to contradict one another but that is precisely the essence of the hero's journey: achieving a goal through surrender.

As an example I would like to mention again the film *Pretty Woman* to show that there is nothing mysterious about this. About a quarter of the way into the film the rich man Edward Luis invites the prostitute Vivian to spend a week as his professional companion. Her answer to this is: "I will be so nice to you that you will never let me go again." The film character Vivian has named the goal she will pursue throughout the film. She wants to have Edward all to herself. How does she manage this? Through achievement, manipulation and calculation? By bursting with niceness and reading his every wish from his lips? No, Vivian freaks out, packs her things in midstream, she provokes him, accuses him to his face of being a cynical businessman, she doubts him–and herself. She is not nice but she is authentic. She stands by her feelings, she stands by what she is. She lives, she surrenders. From this process love emerges. That is how they find one another.

That is exactly how it is with horses. If you want to achieve a goal with a horse, refined technique is only of limited value. It is better to establish a connection. You ask the horse whether it is ready, ask how it feels and you become aware of its signals. You ask yourself whether you are ready. You ask how you are and how things stand with your body-mind-soul-feeling-system.

Then you concentrate on your goal and you both set off. When you are underway, you keep your goal in mind just like your mutual feelings and your connection. That is surrender.

Not an easy task. Especially for people who proceed from the idea that horses, fellow human beings and their environment, are there for them to dominate. For people who neither really perceive themselves nor others.

To treat a horse as a partner rather than a dressage object can produce a host of eureka effects. Instead of hurling theories around as to why my horse is difficult, I could simply consult it. My riding instructor Astrid had such an experience with a gelding she was doing free longeing work with. Like many horses in this situation

Schuppi repeatedly pushed into the centre of the circle. Why are you doing that? she asked him. She suddenly read in his expression real regret. "I would like to do what you require but I simply can't escape from my habit. Will you give me another chance?" Astrid relaxed and a few rounds later the problem was solved.

Horses give us many kinds of hints about how they want to be treated. Often the information from the horse contradicts the tips we have read in how-to books. Their advice refers to horses in general. But each horse is unique and what is gold for one horse is poison for another. Sometimes even your esteemed teacher's advice is wrong. It is up to you. You have to know, feel, decide what is best for you and your horse. This also includes the decision not necessarily to accept the teacher's advice.

Julia wanted to get her horse to go into the trailer. For weeks she had been practising every time she went riding. After a while the mare had become so trusting that she put her forelegs onto the ramp. But there was still a long way to go. Reinhold, a pal of hers from the stable, told her that Pat Parelli could get any horse into a trailer within half an hour—and Julia felt she was a failure. Reinhold was just back from a workshop, so she handed him the rope. He unpacked his newly-acquired Parelli stick and applied steps one, two and three of the Parelli method. The Haflinger Bella grew increasingly panicky. Reinhold felt he had to prove something, drew back the rope and lashed Bella's back with it. Bella reared up, tore free of her halter and ran off as if pursued by the Furies. It was weeks before Julia managed to get her anywhere near a trailer again. "I knew from the beginning it would go wrong but I felt stupid because my own training method was so ineffectual."

Was it really ineffectual? Perhaps the slow tempo was just right for Bella and Julia because it suited their ability level. Our ambition often gets in the way–especially with horses.

The problem with the fourth step of the hero's journey, which involves establishing and realizing a goal, is that having a goal immediately awakens our ambition. This does not mean that a goal is something negative. A goal gives us a structure, it is something very useful. When ambition acquires its own momentum it becomes dangerous. When it cuts us off from our feelings, our self-awareness and other peoples' awareness. Then the process begins to stiffen up, creativity dies. By ignoring her inner voice Julia forfeited all her hard-earned progress.

My mare Tinnia is afraid of water. But all the trails around her new stable crossed some stream or other. After two hours desperately trying to urge her over a runnel, a mere trickle of water, circling and leaving her no way out, it occurred to me to ask her, to ask the horse. You do not have to be an animal communicator to do that, you just have to stop charging at the wall for a moment.

Just leave me in peace, was my horse's understandable answer. I released the reins and she immediately turned and marched straight back to the stable. A few days later I rode to that runnel again and, following my four-legged friend's instructions, I left her in peace. She wanted to be involved in the decision and now strode confidently over the water.

Step Five
Connection

You have to imagine the hero's journey as a circuit, a circular movement. Or to be even more precise: a spiral. When you have reached the end of the circuit, a new one begins on a different level.

The hero's journey is a basic movement in all living creatures. It is never-ending. When you have finished one journey, completed a stage of development, a new journey begins. But for the present we are in the middle of this one.

Our consciousness is not particularly well-trained to think in symbols. That is a deficiency compared to the way our ancestors perceived the world. Because symbols are the gateway to our soul, they are the language of the soul. Through symbols we gain access to the energy and wisdom of nature.

Many people feel attracted to the cultures of Native Americans, of the Celts, the Teutonic tribes, Indian, Chinese and other primitive peoples, because these cultures perceive their world in a symbolic way, in the language of the soul. And because our soul wants to acquire a means of expression, because it wants to communicate with us.

The hero's journey presents the structure, the drama of this soul language. It resembles a ritual. The hero's journey exists in various forms and in varying numbers of steps. It does not depend on how many steps there are. What is important is the descent into the world of the soul, into the night world or what the Celts called the 'other' world. What is important is the encounter with the death of the Ego and with birth, the development of a new consciousness.

I work with the hero's story in eleven steps because for me they represent the essence.

We have now reached the fifth of these eleven steps. The first four represented departure and defined the direction. We establish who we are (our strengths and weaknesses), what drives us forwards (our call to adventure), what we have as luggage (our wounds), and which direction we want to pursue (the goal).

We are on our way across the steppes accompanied by a herd of free-moving horses. The steppes belonged to horses long before man appeared on the map of creation. The eohippus, the oldest-known form of the species 'horse' is 50 million years old. 45 million years later the horse encountered the first human being, who used it as food. Only 5 million years later did he first sit on the horse's back, some 6000 years ago.

From then on the relationship between humans and horses developed rapidly. It was the horse which—until recently—drove the development of human culture decisively forwards.

I mention these developments to give you some grasp of the dimensions involved. Not only human beings but also horses have a collective consciousness. In trance states many people gain access to long-past ages of human existence.

In a vision I myself saw a tribe I belong to, a group of nine people who have sent me to perform a task. This tribe is more than 2000 years old and lives in a cave. Horses, too, carry within them such collective memories, says Linda Kohanov. First the horse provided man with food, then it became his god and spiritual companion, then his labourer and his weapon of war. Today the horse is an item of sports equipment and a leisure companion. Yet gradually it is also becoming man's soul mate again.

When we listen to it with our intuition, we hear ancient stories of sacrifice and initiation. Then we hear of its true greatness. The hero's journey is one way of achieving that. Why do I mention these collective processes of consciousness?

If we want to understand what is taking place in our psyche, beyond the border of awareness, we have to internalise these concepts. For all indigenous peoples their relationship to their ancestors is the basis of social equilibrium. Primitive peoples use the collective knowledge that their ancestors offer them. When we accompany the horse onto the steppes, we enter the collective unconscious not only of our own species but also that of the species equus. And we can make use of their wisdom just as our forefathers used that of their ancestors.

In this fifth step it is a question of our relationships, of the group we belong to, of friendship, love and family. No one undergoes the journey alone. Every living being is related to all other living beings. Step Five involves becoming aware of our relationships. Of finding out what we can learn about relationships from sensitive herd animals.

I would like you to look more closely at a relationship in your life, one which now, at this very moment, is important. Perhaps this relationship has no great significance in your life as a whole, or then again perhaps it does. It is preoccupying you now. The key is the present. Write it down.

Only the moment is alive. Only in the moment can we be creative. Whoever tries to teach a horse something, discovers how quickly horses learn. Just one experience is enough and they have grasped it. Once you have turned up at the fence with a carrot, the horse will ask for another carrot the next day. Once your horse has thrown you and found relieve, it will try to again.

When you have solved a conflict in a relationship, it remains solved. It will not repeat itself in the same form. Nothing repeats itself. You cannot enter the same river twice. Every moment is new and offers you a chance to establish a connection. In relationships it is a question of making connections. Together we enter a river which carries us onward.

Think of the relationship which is important to you at this moment. What feelings does it arouse in you? What needs? What is missing? What makes you happy? Then put yourself in the other person's position. How does he or she feel? What needs does he or she have? What makes him or her happy?

I will introduce you to an encounter which is used in equine-assisted therapy, equine-assisted learning. Imagine a round pen (a fenced-in circle). In the round pen stands a horse. Clearly, instead of a horse you have a book before you, but you will get an idea of what an authentic moment is, and what processes you go through to attain that.

What happens in your relationship with the horse also happens in your relationships with people. Horses teach us to enter into authentic relationships, into relationships which heal us.

Now I will describe Sara's case in altered form to protect her identity. I have also changed her name. It is not important who Sara is. Many women have similar conflicts to Sara's.

I will briefly sum up Sara's story. She no longer loves her husband. She even despises him and has also told him so. She has a new lover whom she meets in secret and she has three adolescent children. Furthermore she owns two horses which are housed in a stable. Her husband is wealthy, she has no income of her own. Her husband has just disclosed to her today that he has fallen in love with another woman. He wants Sara to move out and his new partner to move in and take care of the children, together with her own two children.

Sara is panic-stricken. She is shaking like a leaf. She stands with her back to the round pen. I ask her to concentrate on her body, to scan herself from top to toe. She says that her stomach feels like a pulsing ball of pain. "Ask your pain for information," I suggest. The question is aimed at gaining information from our bodies. Our bodies live in reality, they lead us back into what is real, when our minds have lost their anchorage.

"I am frightened."

"What are you frightened of?"

"Of dying."

I ask Sara to turn to Tinnia. The mare has approached, curious.

"Has your pain changed now that you have turned to Tinnia?"

"The horse frightens me–although normally I'm not frightened of horses. It seems to me to be nervous and I feel too weak to calm it down."

"Ask the horse if it has anything to tell you."

Sara stands there for some time, then she bursts into tears. "I can't. Not today. I'd have to concentrate far too much, but …"

"Take a deep breath. Stay in your body. What can you feel?"

Sara calms down slightly. "I don't know whether it means anything but I feel energy in my feet."

"Ask your feet for information."

Sara looks at me in despair. "How can I do that?"

"What are your legs and your feet telling you?"

Sara bursts into tears again. "But that's not possible. My feet can't speak."

"What would your feet say if they could?"

Sara sighs. "I think this energy in my feet means something, like having both feet on the ground… something like having roots."

"Is that a good feeling?"

"Yes, but it has got nothing to do with my present life."

"But you're feeling it now, aren't you, at this very moment?"

"Yes…" Sara has a crooked grin on her face. "The horse does not seem to me to be quite so nervous any more either."

Tinnia, the mare, has lowered her head but is still watchful.

"What about your fear, has it changed?"

"Not much. I feel I'm choking because my whole situation is so dreadful and I …"

I interrupt Sara who is just about to lose herself again in her pain. "What about your fear of Tinnia?"

"I'm no longer frightened of her. Actually I find peace and security with horses. It's always been like that."

"Are you ready to go into the round pen?"

"Yes," Sara says in a shaky voice.

"Do you want to take a crop with you in case you feel threatened by Tinnia?"

Sara decides on a rope because in her work with horses that is what she normally uses. Then she goes into the ring.

What happens in the round pen is between Sara and Tinnia. I am only there for safety reasons, in case the horse becomes anxious or assertive. I also observe the process so that afterwards I can present to Sara my impressions as feedback.

The horse offers its emotional, physical and spiritual experience.

The process is very subtle and hardly perceptible from outside. "Horses are so sensitive," says Mark Rashid, the American horseman, "so incredibly sensitive that we are light-years away from what they can do."

"People expect something extraordinary to happen," says Carol

Roush, an experienced trainer, who works closely with Linda Kohanov, "but the processes are barely visible to the naked eye." If we go with the process, we perceive a lot with our senses, our bodies and our intuition, and some things are astonishing.

What I see while Sara is in the ring with Tinnia is this: the mare repeatedly nudges Sara with her head, friendly but decisive. Sara shies away with Tinnia annoyingly dogging her every step. Sara is struggling with herself. Apparently she feels too weak to resist Tinnia. She retreats to the edge of the round pen. Tinnia follows her insistently, so that I am close to intervening, the horse has wedged Sara in. But I still want to hold back for a moment because I know Tinnia and how as a rule she never does anything threatening. She is trying to show Sara something.

Suddenly Sara loses control. "Get away!" she shouts, but the horse does not react. Sara remembers the rope in her hand, lashes out at Tinnia and the mare runs off shocked. Sara is sorry she has tried to hit the mare. She holds her hand to her mouth as if she had done something bad. Then she bursts into tears again. She runs to the mare and wants to hug her but Tinnia resists and runs off. Sara stands totally lost in the centre of the ring. Tinnia has turned away and is watching the horses in a distant corral.

For a long time Sara stands there in the centre, indecisive, she seems desperate. Then she wraps her arms around her body as if she wants to hold herself tight. It moves me to watch this. I sense that she has located an authentic feeling. Tinnia seems to have noticed this as well, because she goes to Sara and rests her head on her shoulder. "Thank you," I hear Sara whisper.

She comes out of the round pen. "O my God."

After we have found ourselves two folding chairs I ask, "do you want me to give you some feedback? Or would you prefer to share what you experienced first?".

"I have to tell you what happened," Sara answers excitedly. "Have to just get it out before I forget … so that I trust myself," she stammers, pressing her hands to her mouth.

"Could you tell me in the order things occurred?"

"If I can… Well, first Tinnia pushed me around and I thought 'yes, that's what my life's like', I always get pushed around, or I allow myself to be pushed around. And now, because of this whole situation which I caused myself, things have got so bad that I have no resistance any more. A while ago I had a strong urge to break out of my monotonous marriage. My husband is very… domineering. Everything has to be as he wants it to be. I simply couldn't go on. Everything bristled in me. But I didn't know how to rebel. Then I met Volker, an artist, he is independent, passionate, he lives as I always wanted to live. He is free … with him I feel as I normally only do with the horses. I thought: what are you doing with your life? Surely you have a right to be happy. I didn't dare tell my husband about Volker because I was afraid of his reaction. But I told him that I could no longer bear him to touch me."

Sara starts to cry. "Somehow I knew that all along and I was not surprised when Tinnia pushed me around. The crazy thing was I suddenly realized that in his way Volker was pushing me around just the same. He is simply very strong, he's a strong person, and I have nothing to resist him with. I always thought that he was my liberator but actually with him I feel just as miserable and dependent. It's dreadful to realize that. Then, when Tinnia crowded me right to the edge of the ring, I suddenly remembered that I had the rope— and could defend myself. My reaction was so strong that I drove

Tinnia away. I felt sorry and I wanted to apologize but she didn't accept my apology. Somehow I could understand that. I'm the kind of person who is always apologizing for what they do. To my mind she was saying to me: don't be so feeble, stand by what you did. You drove me away, I can cope with that. But I don't like the way you cringe."

Sara's face lights up and she has that crooked grin again. "I felt she was right. It's so pathetic to squirm like that. Afterwards I felt completely lost. I thought of my children and what I am doing to them, and all the despair came back up. And the only thing I could think of was to hug myself." Sara's whole body begins to shake. "It's all so dreadful."

She holds herself tight again. "I suddenly became aware that I've never done that before. Hug myself. And it felt good. I mean me, poor little defenceless me. Nobody has ever hugged me like that before, not even Volker, and it came as a tremendous insight: this is the beginning. For the first time in my whole life I experienced my Self. And then Tinnia came and put her head on my shoulder." Sara begins to cry uncontrollably. "As if she wanted to tell me: you're ok. That's so incredible. I've ruined my life … and my family's … Can it really be that I'm ok?"

It takes a long time before Sara calms down. "I don't believe any human being could have convinced me of that. I wouldn't have believed them. I find it hard to accept that a horse can tell me something like that but I felt it. It was really there."

"What about your fear of dying?"

"It's gone."

Sara asked me if she could stay on her own with Tinnia for a bit longer. When she said good-bye to me later, she said she had had a long conversation with Tinnia. She had learned from her how she could gain support from her own horses. Tinnia had said, "you have to listen to them."

The moment in which we engage in a vital relationship can change everything. Not only do we make an external connection, we also connect with our own true self. Our true self produces healing.

Every one of us has the power to heal himself and to be healed, to heal others and to be healed by others. Healing comes from connection. That is all. Horses establish this connection with us. They show us when we have found it. Then they become gentle, turn to us. Then they talk to us and their expressive power is astonishing.

The moment we connect we are creative. Creativity means nothing more than connecting with the flow of life. It means re-finding something which we knew as children: play. When we play, we find solutions. Then we take the next step. When we succeed in freeing ourselves from result-oriented thinking, we realize that it is all about process, about taking the next step and that in this way it is easier to attain results. From a straight line a three-dimensional pattern emerges with several layers and dimensions which create an intricate order.

Sara made progress when she realized how she really felt about her new lover, that the freedom he promised was an illusion. That Volker was interested in his own freedom, not hers. For Sara it was an important experience to connect with her feelings and to find out that this was where the solution to her problems lay.

It is true that her female friends had already told her that Volker was not the right man for her but she had to feel it for herself. Just as she had to feel who this genuine Sara was who felt stifled by life.

When we confront a horse, ideally our whole existence comes together: our feelings, our body, our mind and our soul. Horses demand this from us. And there is no greater satisfaction than when a gracious, power-packed, million-year-old, independent and highly sensitive animal, weighing some 600 kilos, tells us that we are whole and perfect now.

How is it possible for a horse to talk to us?

Each one of us is involved in an infinitely extended web of relationships with our contemporaries, our ancestors, with animals, plants, with every living thing. We weave this web night and day, in our waking state and in sleep.

The biologist, Rupert Sheldrake, calls this web a morphogenetic field. Many ancient spiritual doctrines speak of this: the Indian Akasha Chronicles, for example. Quantum Theory discovered some hundred years ago that observer and experiment are interdependent, that there is no reality independent of our subjective participation. Science keeps finding more and more incredibly complicated processes which confirm what primitive people grasped intuitively: that all things are inter-related.

A network of countless connections defines our existence. Some bring us joy, some pain. If the connection is present, pain is recognizable as illusion, as entanglement from which the authentic moment frees us. Our relationships serve to free us. We become entangled in order to reach through entanglements to freedom, to that true connection which is love.

It is beyond our imaginings how powerful and interwoven this

91

web really is. Sometimes we catch a glimpse, sometimes the veil is torn open and we see how multi-layered things are, from the most banal right up to the mythical level, from our personal history to the history of the collective in which it is embedded.

The consolation is that we cannot fall out of this net. The Indians speak of this experience when they say that we are all one: Mitakuye Oyasin.

A postcard of Hadban Enzahi had me dreaming of Arabian horses. Years later such a horse of real flesh and blood entered my life and became a gateway for my soul. Tinnia–and I hardly noticed this to start with–took me with her on a hero's journey.

Horses opened my eyes to the significance of my work, of writing. A year ago I asked Yvonne Monahan's horse, Cisco, whether I should seriously consider becoming an author of spiritual texts. At that time this seemed to me a strange option. Cisco wrinkled his nostrils and gave me an arrogant look. You've long known that, he said to me. Even today, after many such experiences, what then happened to me still seems strange. But why should my mind not be free to wonder? After all the poor thing has been trained for forty years to explain its world in every detail.

I have to learn to give myself, my mind, my contemporaries time to grasp this idea. I am frightened of being considered odd, naïve or even insane by my fellow human beings. But the truth, once recognized, cannot be forgotten. And love is always present. We each of us have our task. We are never alone.

When people start to really see themselves, their true centre, they invite others to drop their masks, too, give up their cynicism and treat themselves with more compassion.

To be a horse in human form is infectious. The more we absorb the wisdom of horses the more we carry it into our towns and densely populated areas, to people who do not know the smell of a horse's sweat and have never been splashed by the mud of a horse galloping by. But perhaps a postcard of Hadban Enzahi is thrust into some girl's hand and she feels her heart beating wildly within her. Our memory of horses will continue to carry us for a long time, even now that they no longer seem to have a place in our time any more. Our common history is too old. And possibly it really is horses that can heal us.

"We are extinguishing life because we deceive ourselves about its character. We treat it so cruelly because we consider it to be machinery, junk. As nature lies dying, so do our feelings. Our understanding of living creatures will decide the future for us", writes biologist Andreas Weber in his book *Alles fühlt* (Everything has Feelings).

If we ourselves want to be healed, we have to heal the history we have shared with horses. I feel that I have become part of this task. By that I do not mean that we owe horses something. Guilt is a feeling that horses have no conception of. The matter goes much deeper, is much more archaic. To really understand it, we have to go back to the myths, where human and equine consciousness was not yet split. Although human beings have inflicted endless suffering on horses, it is not our task to ask their forgiveness, or to put them on a pedestal and worship them. Horses want nothing from us and have never wanted anything from us other than that we become whole and return to ourselves. It is not horses we need to heal, it is ourselves.

Caroline Morgan, riding instructor and dressage rider, summed this up for me when she said, "now I realize that I do not need to improve my relationship to horses but to myself."

Horses, the whole of nature, are interested in healing and we human beings are part of that. It is our natural condition. By becoming conscious of our history with horses, we become conscious of how we are estranged from ourselves, and by becoming conscious of that we overcome our alienation.

Human beings feel this necessity. Why else should there be three times more horses today than when we made them work for us, although keeping horses is expensive, time-consuming and difficult? Although horses are only used for pleasure in our spare time? Horses still play a major role in the development of our culture. They point us in the direction we have to move, where solutions and our future lie.

Horses want us to cross over to the other side, in order to recognize the true nature of our relationships.

"If men and women could find their centre in the Tao, the whole world would be transformed according to its natural rhythms. People would be content with their simple every-day lives, in harmony and free of desire," it says in the more than 2700-year-old Tao Te Ching.

Once we have started seeing through horses' eyes, we will find traces everywhere. And they always point to the same wisdom.

I have constantly wondered where my mare Tinnia's name comes from. That is what she was called when I bought her.

Recently, in one of our conversations, which in the meantime have become a habit with us, Tinnia insisted that I go to the Württemberg Landesmuseum in Stuttgart. There an important research detail for my novel about the Celts was awaiting me, but not only that: I discovered an explanatory plaque in the archaeological department dealing with the main Etruscan deity. The name of this deity was: Tinnia! I was astonished.

A different trail was revealed when I was recently phoning my father. It turned out that the two cast-iron horses' heads I like on a house façade I had been driving past for the last forty years, belonged to my great-grandfather who was a master saddler and had been one of the Blue Dragoon. His house was destroyed in the war, the horses' heads ended up in strange hands in a different town and ultimately on that house front from which they had so often greeted me. Only now did I discover this connection to my great-grandfather.

When we become receptive to the great network, our life becomes filled with such messages and connections. I keep a diary to remind myself that I have actually experienced many such unusual things.

This book, too, arose from similar messages and occurrences. For me there is great consolation in the dream messages horses send me, in which they assure me that I have no need to worry because they will accompany the book on its way out into the world. It is just as much their book as it is mine.

I am sure you know such stories from your own life. When the subject of horses comes up in conversation, almost everyone has a story to tell. The stories tell of relationships right across time, they tell of death and the beyond, of accidents, dangers, faithfulness and of great love. It is now time for you to tell your story. You have two tasks to perform for this stage of the journey.

The first task is: what stories do you have about horses? You will find yourself in these stories. Take a close look at them and try to hear the horses' messages. Write your story down and look for its message.

The second task: I have asked you to think of a relationship which you are involved in at the moment. Now go to your horse in the stable or out in the field–if possible go alone with your horse to the riding arena, to the round pen or some other fenced-off area. Let the relationship you are thinking of manifest itself in your body, that is: concentrate on it and feel the tension produced in you.

Ask this place in your body for a feeling. How do you feel in your relationship? Then turn to your horse and go back into your body. Try to find a connection with your horse and at the same time concentrate on the relationship preoccupying you.

Observe your horse's reactions. Observe how your feelings change and how your horse in turn reacts to that. Follow the process until you feel it has reached a conclusion. You will know when the tension has dissolved and you are calm and present within yourself.

It is not always easy to find the message this resolution brings. Keep at it. Pay attention to your horse. When the process is over, go through it once more in your thoughts and write it down, that will help you become conscious of how your feelings proceed.

Try to work through two such emotional processes on different issues. The second process does not necessarily have to deal with relationships. It can also revolve around profession-

al decisions or anything else which centres on you yourself.

It is important that you find the connection. Once you have learned to find that, you will always be able to return to it, and your horse will develop into a superb teacher and a major source of advice for you.

I know, this all sounds mysterious which is why I would like to offer you some theory to help you along. Horses naturally seek relaxation and well-being and they find it in their connection with their fellow horses and with other living creatures like, for example, human beings. That applies not only to horses but to all living creatures.

"Organisms are not clockwork consisting of clearly separated elements. They are unified wholes held together by a powerful force: a feeling for what does them good and what harms them," Andreas Weber writes. When we come into contact with horses, they adopt our feelings and reflect them. This phenomenon is familiar to all horse people. In striving to feel good, horses internalize our feelings and earth them. They do not brood endlessly about problems, neither do they get stuck in feelings, their emotions are in constant flux. For horses feelings are information which move them to act in order to produce well-being. We can recognize ourselves in equine behaviour, it mirrors our own. Suddenly we are feeling instead of thinking. Suddenly we are in our bodies instead of in our heads.

It is not our feelings which are a problem but the way we deal with them. That we negate them, repress them or fall victim to them instead of letting ourselves be carried by their flow. Horses bring us back into the flux of our feelings. We relax and the horses come to us, establish a connection and together we feel good. This transfer of feeling takes place, according to new scientific research, through an electro-magnetic field which surrounds our body, that is: not just our brains but our hearts, whose force field is 5000 times greater. Feelings are much stronger bearers of information than thoughts. We are in contact with our environment chiefly through our feelings. Horses bring this awareness back into our lives.

Step Six

The Heart of the Creature

Although horses are large and powerful, they are also vulnerable. And we humans are, too–that is fertile ground for miracles.

The sixth step of the heroic journey marks its centre point. In films this occurs half-way through, similarly in books. Here the most deeply emotional point is reached.

At this point the traveller does not yet find what she has been looking for, but she confronts her deepest desire and she becomes certain that her journey will be borne by this experience. In love stories it is true love. The couple are not yet united, they first have to pass other examinations. But their love is certain and there is no longer any way back. Whoever loves loves. What I know deep within, I know. It is this gut feeling which we meet half way through the journey.

"Some things, as we know deep in our souls, are true, no matter what anybody may say about them," writes Shelley Rosenberg, the successful dressage rider and horse trainer in her book *My Horses, my Healers.*

I have put this quotation at the beginning of my book because it is so apt for what we find at the core of the journey.

It is not a question of what I tell you in this book or what anybody tells you. It depends on what you know and believe.

Only love is certain, my mare once told me. This is my profoundest conviction. Our profoundest conviction is not an insight produced by the intellect, our profoundest conviction is something that satisfies our whole existence: body, mind, feelings and spirituality.

Such deeply-felt knowledge gives us a power, which enables us to bear much. Christian martyrs have sacrificed their lives for that. Such knowledge has transcended the ages in many forms, in the *Tao Te Ching* and in other spiritual teachings. Such knowledge gives us a strong hold, an anchorage in life.

In former times people were fully immersed in systems of belief, in which they found such knowledge. Nowadays we live in an individualized society, where many go in search of such knowledge independently. A search, which has occupied people since time immemorial and which is one of humanity's most fundamental and noble goals.

Once you have seen and felt how infinitely gentle and sensitive the creature horse is, you can no longer do certain things. Once people realized what it does to a child when it is beaten, they stopped beating children. Once people realized that coloured slaves had the same feelings as they had, they freed slaves. Once people realized that all human beings have the same rights to live and determine their own lives, they set a revolution in motion.

The sixth step of the heroic journey is an initiation. I spoke earlier about the heroic journey in films, but now I'll take it one step further. In films the heroic journey mostly only reaches the emotional level. An initiation however is concerned with a breakthrough into a region beyond everyday consciousness. In modern psychology it is called the transpersonal area. Primitive peoples developed rituals for that. In our western society the connection to this transpersonal area has largely been lost and with it a part of our human potential.

I cannot create an initiation experience for you in a book such as this, but I can describe to you what it consists of and where you can possibly find it.

Our perception and our experiences are shot through with the transpersonal often without us being aware of it. Every dream is a transpersonal experience. If we learn to read its message, we learn something about our true self. That other region contains information and wisdom vital to life. Meditation offers further access, prayer, art—and the conscious contact with horses.

"There is a wide range of old as well as Eastern practices which are especially intended to make access to the transpersonal region easier. The whole spectrum of experience has been described by historians, anthropologists and scholars of comparative religion, together with various Shamanic procedures, rites of passage and the healing ceremonies of primitive peoples, death and rebirth mysteries as well as trance dancing in ecstatic religions. More recent consciousness research created for the first time a genuine synthesis of centuries-old wisdom and modern science," writes the

American psychiatrist and consciousness researcher Stanislav Grof in his book *The Adventure Of Self-Discovery—Healing Through Changed States Of Consciousness.*

Genuine initiation contains the four realms of human existence: they are often divided up into Earth (body), Water (feelings), Air (thinking) and Fire (spirituality). When all these areas come together, a powerful transformation occurs.

The adolescent Indian withdraws into the wilderness for three days and there acquires a new name, the name of his soul, which is revealed to him by a spirit from the other world. He is given his life task. He recognizes his place in the community.

In the initiation into becoming a true horse person, that is what I'll call it here, you recognize the true essence of horses. Once you have recognized it, you can confront horses freely. Then you will gain their voluntary cooperation, you will be able to play with them and really dance.

The mustang Sundance was being brought to Vera in Switzerland but he died in transport. His death changed her life because she understood what was really important to her. She no longer wanted to work in a bank but help people find their own means of expression. This was her highest goal, that was where she found her true self.

Britta bought herself a Friesian gelding after it became clear to her that she was too old to have children. Her relationships with men had not been very successful. She longed for a creature to whom she could give all her love, someone who would not desert her. Soon she bought a Frisian mare as well and had her mated. She fell out with the stable owner, hired a plot of land and established her own stable. She established credit to be able to build the stable.

The mare's pregnancy proved complicated, the foal was born too early and could only be kept alive at high veterinary cost. Nevertheless Britta gave her all in looking after the foal.

Then, however, in a round of company redundancies she lost her job as a chemist. She soon ended up in financial difficulties given the cost of the horses' upkeep and had to sell her flat. Some time later the horses as well. Being separated from her horses plunged Britta into deep depression. She could no longer even make an effort to go for an interview for a new job. She was convinced that she would never get what she was searching for in life, that is: lasting love.

One day Britta visited a friend who was doing an unpaid job in an animal home. She understood that it was not a question of being loved but of being needed by some other living being. That very same day she joined the organization. The work gave her new energy and she began to put her life back together.

How far have you got on your journey? Has a door opened for you? Do you feel afraid of looking into the eye of the storm? Are you torn between turning round and going on? The heart of the creature, the centre of the journey, is no comfortable seat by a crackling fire. At the heart of the creature there blows a strong wind, the world goes up in flames, there are floods, the earth sinks in rot and decay. Before anything new can be born, old things must die.

To advance to this place requires courage. Because this is where you confront your greatest fear. My friend Andrea calls it walking through fire.

Who are you really? What do you really desire? And what ghosts lurk in the dark? What causes you such fear? Name both your greatest wish and your greatest fear. Now.

Since I have been on this journey, my life is a maelstrom. One day I received a weird, but appropriate image for it. Me sitting in a boat made of banana skins.

Looking into the eye of a horse, into the heart of the creature can reveal profound truth which slowly begins to restructure your life. Once you have seen the truth, you cannot go back. You can postpone it, repress it, but you cannot forget it.

For some people this is the beginning of a fear-choked path. But what is this fear in comparison to what comes to light. We will find our true self, the one place where there is security and trust.

What a blessing to know that there is such a path at all, says the spiritual teacher Ram Dass.

An English riding instructor gives up her career to visit all the horse people whose books have impressed her, Linda Kohanov, Alexander Nevzorov, Carolyn Resnick, Mark Rashid. After she has seen what is possible, she can no longer go back to her usual life.

"It is humiliating to see how my pupils move to other teachers," she says in the documentary film about her experiences: *The Path of the Horse.*

During my training program with Linda Kohanov in Arizona I met several people who from one day to the next could not go on. "Time and again I suddenly broke into tears," says a former successful tournament rider. "First the people in our stable wondered what was wrong with me, then they got used to it."

It is a process modern society does not prepare us for. In ancient cultures this spiritual way was embedded in rituals which protected the travellers. Psychotherapy and traditional religion can only partially soften the blows.

What happens on this journey does not take place within a psychological, nor in a traditional Christian framework. It is a creaturely, spiritual, transpersonal process and can only be carried out and can only lead to healing on this plain. I am not a psychotherapist nor a cleric, but I am a lifelong artist. In the theatre I learned what authenticity means. My own fire walk has been full of potholes, roller coaster rides and never-ending storms. There I found something in myself which I call Stormrider.

The Indian Spirit Seeker Phillip Whiteman Jr. speaks of the power of the buffalo, a creature which is worshipped by the Indians for being able to dive into the storm and come out again at the other end. My storm rider energy is something similar. My familiarity with creative work helps me survive transpersonal storms, because creativity and spirituality are similar in many respects. Writing the way I do it is spiritual practice.

You do not need to be an artist to undertake the journey. We each of us make the journey in our own way, with the abilities we have trained for, and the strengths we possess naturally. We are all on a journey already, whether we are aware of it or not. Because it begins at birth, and perhaps even before that.

Ram Dass, formerly a Harvard professor, tells of someone who attended one of his highly spiritual lectures. The lady sat in the first row, wearing a Chanel suit and a hat decorated with artificial flowers, so she was completely out of place amidst the bearded, Rasta-haired hippy audience of the 70s. Nonetheless the lady nodded eagerly at his every word. When he later asked her how she clearly gained such insights as others only found on LSD trips, her answer was: from crochet work.

Had he heard correctly? Yes, crocheting. It came to him that it is not a question of the activity but of the attitude with which it is performed.

Is there an activity in your life which produces a meditative condition in you? If you ride or own horses, perhaps it is riding or your work with your horse. Which activities or arts have a meditative character for you? Draw up a list and describe the activity in a few words. Can you recognize in it a spiritual practice which you were unaware of before?

Meditation or processes of consciousness are not a normal part of everyday conversation amongst riders. When I meet horse people, I am interested in their emotional experiences with horses. I often hear moving stories. I have never met a single horse person who does not know intuitively what horses give him. Most of them have not yet thought about what it exactly is that draws them to horses and why they are so refreshed when they return from the stable.

Jutta, a former tournament rider, told me: "During my law study I reached a point where I wanted to give it all up, I saw no way of being able to manage the huge work load. I was no longer even sure about whether I wanted to go into law, did not even know what else I could do. I was going through a major crisis. I had even lost all enthusiasm for tournament riding, I was even already won-

106

dering whether to sell my horse, a wonderfully endearing Hanove-
rian mare.

I withdrew for a week in order to think things over, to do nothing, to remove the pressure and to see what would happen if I was
free of external obligations. And what did I do that week? Every
morning after coffee I was drawn to the stable. But not to ride cir-
cles in the arena. No, I took Alexa for a walk. We walked around
the area for hours on end. I had never done that before. What happened on these walks was weird. In her presence my thoughts, my
chaotic feelings spontaneously began to find some order. When I
went home, I felt calmer and a bit better every day. At the end of
the week I felt so grateful to my horse. I could not believe Alexa
had done that for me–and yet, I knew it was her who had done it. I
had realized that I did not study law to become a lawyer and bend
the law but because I have a strong sense of justice."

Today Jutta works as a judge. "Being with my horse," she says,
"gives me the strength for it."

Even if the fire walk, the heroic journey, is a path into the dark,
incalculable zone of our psyche, a part of the way consists of something very down to earth: work. An activity which we repeat time
and again as we slowly acquire an ability. My friend Tina says about
it: "It is as if you owned an enormous house and had to scrub all
on your own every room, every awkward corner and every box
room on hands and knees–till everything is spick and span."

You may also be working on learning an instrument, a sport or a
language. It can be mucking out your stable. The practice helps you
to reach the point where your inner wisdom is revealed.

Remember the card you drew, or the motto you found for
achieving your aim (step 4). Perhaps here you will find an element

which inspires you to regular activity and practice. Constant repetition of the same activity is a gateway to that place where you meet your true self. The revelation need not come with a bang. Often it comes quietly and gradually. Your life changes almost unnoticed.

Perhaps you know that from working with horses. You practice something over and over again and suddenly your horse has learned a new movement, figure, or ability and it seems changed, not only physically, but also mentally.

There are many roads and many countries that can be travelled. Decisive is not what, but how.

For horses that makes all the difference. When you observe a true horseman or horsewoman, you will find that in many respects they do what every other rider or horse trainer does. If you observe how quickly Monty Roberts or Pat Parelli persuade a frightened horse to go into a trailer, the essential thing is hardly noticeable. What is essential is the inner attitude.

Can you discern a development in your meditative activity? Have you ever experienced a breakthrough doing it, either once or more often? In retrospect, can you tell whether anything fundamental in your life has changed?

If you consciously engage in this process, there comes a moment at some time or other when you reach a new level. You cannot master this way just with energy and exertion alone. Neither can you cope with it with just your mind. Your path leads through the country beyond the border, behind the curtain. There forces reign which are greater than yourself. You can use them. All you have to do is surrender, have faith.

Perhaps you are already on your journey and are not aware of it. Only in retrospect do you recognize individual lines. Recognize the stages of the heroic journey which you have already been on. In our lives we make several great heroic journeys. Becoming an adult, finding true love, the birth of a child, intensely pursuing a career, suffering an illness … any of these can constitute a heroic journey.

So, what awaits you at the heart of the journey? You find your true self, your calling, your life task. But you do not just pick it up like some treasure by the roadside. If it were so simple, you would have found yourself long ago. In our world bristling with offers and temptations you can apparently find everything if you are ready to dish out the necessary banknotes. For the treasure that you find in step six of the heroic journey the stakes are higher. Your stake is you yourself.

Do you know the story of Job, the rich man in the Bible from whom everything was taken away to test his faith?

Does your horse come to you when you go into the corral to collect it? Or are you so intent on catching it, that it shies away from your intention and runs off? Do people withdraw from you because they feel your determination to monopolize, use or even cheat them? Are you unable to pacify your new-born child and do you become more and more desperate? Do men or women you are in love with reject you, do they leave or deceive you? Where does the weakness come from that takes you over when you go to that place at the centre, when you go into the heart of the creature which is your own heart?

At the heart of the creature you are weak, totally weak. And the weaker you are, the stronger you will become. That is the law of the journey. This step is its centre. Weakness requires courage. Being weak is an important ability.

I am weak. It is true, I still have the strength I had before. But I have lost the will to apply it. I can no longer endlessly change my books according to someone else's will. Not since I have understood that a book has its own essence, its own soul, which I, the author, have to protect. That is not some sort of ego-trip. I only recognized it after I handed over my ego at the gate.

At this place many things are reversed. It is as if I was seeing a negative of the world, from behind, from below, standing on its head.

Once you have realized that you have to change in order to get closer to your horse, everything else in your life changes. Horses are a symbol of the way we deal with our fellow beings, our work and ourselves.

It took a long time for me, as an author, to understand that I am part of the text. In the conventional understanding which we have about writing, creativity, our work in general, that hardly ever occurs. There we are gifted specialists who have acquired a specific facility. Likewise in riding. The development of the rider's personality is only ever spoken of on the periphery, if at all. There is much talk about horses being unflustered. But who trains the rider to be relaxed, open, flexible, focused, easy, with rhythm and drive?

I find writing this book quite different to others I've written. I began about ten days ago, the book began me. It comes in waves. I have never thought about it as I did about the others. I feel that it exists as a closed unit and reveals itself step by step. If only I could always write like this!

I only prepared myself energetically, not mentally, for the book. When I read back through my notebook, I find various entries: "Everywhere and continually I see the number 23 ... I can talk to my horse and it gives me names or future events which actually happen ... In my dreams I learn a new way of flying ... An enormous wave-like feeling sweeps over me ... It is as if I had broken through some blockage, I am dragged along and swept away ... Sadness and pain, fear so great that all day long I freeze from within outwards ... I have stomach cramps for days, can hardly eat anything, suffer from neck pains, which no relaxation exercises can release ... I can no longer ride because I am too weak, I go for walks with my horse over freezing cold, snow-covered winter landscapes, wander through lifeless nature, burst into tears, yet am full of overwhelming gratitude and love."

When you have such feelings and they cannot be traced back to a dramatic experience in your life, like separation, losing your job or a bereavement, then you may well be in the middle of a heroic journey.

In Arizona, in Linda Kohanov's Epona Center, I found people who supported me through this crisis, women experienced in spiritual guidance. And intelligent horses.

I found my heart.

I reached a point where I thought I was going to die. Where I could see no way in which I could go on living, when the world around me is so destructive, so masked, so alien and I am a part of it. I was overwhelmed by guilt feelings which I could no longer bear.

At the centre of my hopelessness, the whole scene was transformed and I could see the larger context. Those tortured and maltreated creatures about whom I felt so guilty leant towards me and said, "we will give you life. You are here for us and we are here for you. You bear no guilt." They said, "your first birth is concluded. You will now be born into your higher self." I saw snow-clad mountains. I was alone with a horse as my only companion. Up there the wise woman of the mountains awaited me. I received answers to questions which I had long been asking myself. I saw my life and my death and saw that everything is in perfect order. In one afternoon I was cured of many fears. This book is part of my new path.

In the heart of the creature I saw myself and I was calm. I found trust and love. Fear, despair, hopelessness were simply gateways. They are the storm which tears loose your anchorage, and if you weather it, leads to the light.

The way to the light is not the sunrise on a spring morning, but staying here and looking darkness in the face.

Horses force us to stay here. They buck and rear, they bolt to remind us of the here and now. It is a mistake to think that we ought to correct horses. They correct us.

Where have you arrived at on your journey?

Have you seen the gentleness of horses? Have you found that place of gentleness in yourself and gained an idea of what effect that can have on your life?

Have you experienced how weak you are when you drop everything that is not genuine, your strong performance, your self control, your ego's dreams of omnipotence? As weak as a rider who takes off his horse's bridle and halter and sees it

gallop off. Who sees that he has no power over the horse without his tackle and that the horse does not come back to him voluntarily.

Have you experienced how your horse came to you when you stopped wanting it to, when you waited for it? How it loves its encounters with you, how it welcomes the connection with you when you laugh or cry?

Where have you arrived at on your journey? At the point from which there is no return? What have you found there?

Perhaps you have found words for it, perhaps pictures, perhaps stories you want to share with others. Perhaps silence which you share with your horse, your dog, your cat, a tree, a river, a stream or a cloud? Perhaps an energetic field which you feel time and again, signs which you follow.

Perhaps you have been sucked into a stream of events which push your life in a new direction. Into a storm which has torn out your roots. Perhaps there is suddenly a strength in you which you never knew, which enables you to master every burden.

Is there a force which carries and leads you, even if it takes you to dark places? A force which comes from without and at the same time from within? A force beyond your intellect, which forms you while you rebuild your life?

Do not be impressed by what splendid trips others tell you of. The journey can be very peaceful. Do not think you ought to experience certain things that others have experienced. Your journey is different to everybody else's.

Listen to other people's stories to recognize what they have in common, then forget them and experience your own journey. Find your own creature heart.

On this step of the heroic journey it is up to you how you wish to manifest it. But do manifest it, make it reality, make it visible. It is important for you to know that these things, however unusual, alien and insane they may appear to you, have actually happened. That you have felt and perceived them.

Draw, write, paint, sing, photograph, build, collect ... for you.

You and I, we are all part of a greater whole that feeds and protects us and is focused on healing. Perhaps you have also felt, seen, recognized, experienced that.

Perhaps somebody asks you what has happened to you and you do not have an answer.

You have reached the other side, the land beyond the border. You do not yet know your way about and do not yet have any words for it. It is a place where only you exist, you alone, and whose secret only you can fathom. The secret does not yet have a name which is presentable to the world. When somebody asks you where you are, say: I don't know.

The horses there—you can be sure of that—know when you have arrived there. They bid you welcome.

Step Seven
Contradiction

You have reached the deepest point in yourself, you have found the secret. Even if only for a brief moment–you were there.

But the old self is powerful. Did you merely imagine everything? What use is this experience to you? Can you earn money with it? Will other people like your new self? Will they consider you mad? Or expect proof of your new abilities? Perhaps you think it was quite nice to experience that kind of thing, but now real life goes on. You think: I'll have to see how I get on in everyday life. But then again the journey is so fascinating and you want to go on, take the next step. Nothing is quite so exciting as this journey.

You are now faced with a real test of nerves.

This test removes you from the flow. You are sitting in a boat, rowing forwards with one arm, backwards with the other. The stream of life flows on while you are caught in a contradiction. Two opposed principles, opinions, values, goals tear you apart inwardly.

This internal conflict also reveals itself sooner or later in your external life.

Or life itself dumps an inescapable either-or situation at your feet. You fall in love with two men. You receive an attractive job offer in a different town. You are offered two horses, both perfect yet fundamentally different.

The contradiction presents a situation in which you are forced to choose between two mutually exclusive alternatives. It is a call for individuality. Once we have chosen one alternative, our future will never be the same again. Beforehand the realm of possibilities is still open, afterwards we are confronted with a new reality and all its consequences.

When we get caught up in a contradiction, we have to make sure of our bearings, we have to make decisions instead of being trapped in abstraction, in a vague state of possibility. Horses can make nothing of abstractions. That is a shock for most people when they are first confronted with a horse. Horses do not react to our strategies or our self-righteous evasions. What is most striking to anybody who experiences equine consciousness is the realization that our whole culture lies dozing in a deadly sleep of abstraction.

"As nature lies dying, so do our feelings," writes biologist Andreas Weber in his book demonstrating a radical paradigmatic change in science. He argues that the Darwinian ideology—the mechanistic world view, according to which nature functions like dead clockwork—is based on an error that has devastating consequences for our psyche. When we become further alienated from nature, "we will be psychologically impoverished in a way which was hitherto quite inconceivable. And because soul and body belong together, it will ultimately also have its effects on our real lives."

That single moment, when a horse turns to a person and lays his muzzle on their shoulder, suffices: suddenly the human being understands that this horse actually feels–as he does. He realizes that the horse sees something in him which he himself does not want to believe, but which he is aware of now that the horse has reminded him of it. There comes a moment when old perceptions, the old view of the world lifts its head and he wonders whether he has merely imagined it all. But the wisdom of the heart has awoken in him, and from then on he can no longer forget it.

The next few days he spends in shock. Could he have been so blind? Did he really live his whole life without seeing this truth? What does it mean that horses are not the stupid animals he had considered them to be? That their feelings are so refined, their consciousness in some respects even superior to his? That the very animals he had considered feeble-minded could be his healers, his saviours, these creatures who remind him of the knowledge that implies his survival?

Once this profound recognition comes, the contradiction is unavoidable. Everything must be examined–tempered in fire. Every conviction, every preconception is questioned, a tug of war arises between the old and the new world views. The condition can be unbearable because, like a tipped domino, a fallen thought can start a chain reaction which does not stop until the answer is found.

The recognition that nature really lives and feels, not only because one has fought one's way to religious conviction, but also be-

117

cause one experiences this life as an important force within oneself, can disturb a person's balance.

It is not easy to endure a contradiction. It comes in phases, in waves which affect the whole person. Can I really believe this or that? And how under these circumstances can I continue my previous life?

I DON'T WISH TO KNOW THAT. I DON'T WISH TO FEEL IT. The pain becomes physical, the burden of knowledge unbearable. Human drama.

I have learned from horses that it is our lifelong task to establish a connection to other living beings. We can only establish this connection if there are aspects which can be connected. Two participants must be involved: two people, two horses, a person and a horse. Relationships go wrong when one of the participants is not fully present.

A horse has no alternative to being really there because as potential prey his instincts are directed at survival. A human being is more corruptible. Through education and life experience it can happen that a person withdraws so fully into himself that there are hardly any traces left of his true essence.

Horses react to our essence, not to the behaviour we present up front or that we have adopted for its apparent effectiveness. They continually question whether you are authentic. They do it to find out whether they can trust you. They depend on the social aptitude of other members of the herd. Horses know exactly which of them has the greatest capacity for leadership. And this is the animal they follow.

The leader is not the one with the greatest physical presence, but the one who is most attentive, most balanced. An ego buried under masks and paralysing habits is too slow to be able to react appropriately in a threatening situation. A horse cannot trust such a leader.

Horses train us in mindfulness, a faculty which has an effect on our whole life. Many horse people possess such watchfulness simply by spending a lot of time with horses. When we become more conscious of this attentiveness, it becomes stronger and we can increase our sensitivity. Then we become horses in human form.

In the contradiction phase of our journey we are half present and half absent. Many things succeed surprisingly well, others go wrong. That things go wrong is just as valuable as things going right. We learn the difference between the two.

In our culture the ideal of perfectionism dominates, perfectionism kills our life spirit. It prevents us from taking risks. That is why I love such contradictions. Creativity means trying things out and assuming that 50% of things go wrong, or 99%. Accordingly Edison invented the light bulb by trying out ninety-nine ways in which it did not work.

Perfectionists are mostly cynics. Have you ever noticed that? Possibly in yourself? They are cynics because they despise that human part of themselves which now and again fails.

The poet Rainer Maria Rilke wrote: "The only courage that is demanded of us is the courage to confront the strangest, most uncommon, most inexplicable things that could happen to us. That humanity has been cowardly in this respect has caused endless damage to life."

When you are in the middle of this test of nerves, the perfectionist in you vies with your chaotic but creative side. Can you imagine what horses think about human perfectionists?

You have now acquired some idea of the power within you, some awareness of the being that is you beyond superficialities. In my workshops I take people out for a horseback ride with their eyes closed, with somebody else leading the horse. Afterwards the participants are invited to produce a name for their other self, their soul-self, their creative self. This name they keep to themselves. It is meant for them alone.

You can give yourself such a name. Perhaps you create your own ritual to find it. Or you go to your horse and simply ask for it. I'm sure it has a name for you.

The heroic journey becomes more difficult with every step. That is its law, it is the law of the dramatic, the law of living things. There are no repetitions. As autumn follows summer, so descent follows ascent–and vice versa.

When we submit completely to the law of life, we are part of a stream which carries us forever forwards. There is no standing still, there is only movement. Standing still is artificial. Standing still means that we have been swept into a stagnant by-water and now need a fresh current.

Flow is the goal of our existence. Yesterday I handed over the horse's lead-rope to a friend of mine visiting me from Berlin. I invited her to take a *spirit walk* with Tinnia, a hero's journey with a flesh-and-blood horse.

To begin with it was not easy for Uschi to control my spirited

Arabian mare, especially when other horses appeared on the horizon and Tinnia lifted her tail to impress her fellow horses. Uschi, who had no experience leading horses, could not fall back onto trusted methods and tricks but was completely dependent on her own six senses. I was ready to take over the horse if she or I had the feeling that there was some danger.

The goal Uschi wished for on her hero's journey was to "flow" with the horse. Her wish came true not from dominating the horse and elevating herself to leader, but by completely admitting to herself that the task of leading a horse is damned difficult, that it is hard to unify physical coordination with disturbed feelings and to adjust oneself to the horse and the environment.

Exertion, tension, even grief overwhelmed Uschi when she reached the lowest point on the journey. Describing her experience later Uschi wrote: "Only the sound of the stream rushing by gives me the feeling that everything continues to flow. Now I ask Tinnia what will help me find the creative energy for my journey. At first she pretends to be uninterested in my question ... then she points to my heart."

As if this momentary exchange had appeased the storm in the horse's disturbed body, Tinnia calmed down. Uschi and Tinnia completed the second part of the journey in complete harmony. No professional could have led the horse better over stick-and-stone-strewn ground, over patches of ice, bottlenecks or negotiated the racetrack to the stable.

Uschi goes on to write: "The creative wild energy, which is the driving force for every endeavour, is a power that is difficult to control. That is how the force lying dormant in me at the moment feels. I now know that it's there. I can now communicate to this wild energy that I accept it and allow it to find a place within me. … A day after the spirit walk I became seriously ill. I lay in bed with a high fever and a splitting headache. The following morning, though, I already felt much better again, and by evening it was all gone, I was back to full strength. Another day later I want to go to the skating-rink with my sister. At last the sun is shining, I have a strong desire to go gliding over the ice. Nothing comes of it, however, because for the first time in history a notice at the Dolder skating-rink reads "Tölt at Dolder": the first Icelandic horse tournament is taking place there, the 'Tölt' being the special Icelandic horse's 'ambling' gait. The horses have me back."

The contradiction is resolved the moment we gain access to our authentic selves.

With my mare Tinnia I myself experienced another example of a contradiction, which proceeded as follows:

"My head is buzzing. I have looked into the heart of the creature. I want to continue to follow this powerful road. Shall I start training with Linda Kohanov? It will cost money which I don't have, to earn it implies stress, dependency. Can that be the meaning of it all? I consult my mare as we ride along a lonely forest path. I receive an image: A letter Y and the number 2. Y 2. What is it supposed to mean? I don't understand. A few days later I have an idea. If you consider the letter as a picture, the Y symbolizes a fork in the path. Next to that the number Two. Two paths. I can only take one path. The horse mirrors to me that I am involved in a contradiction. By this time I am no longer surprised that a horse is capable of making such a philosophical statement."

Strictly speaking it is not that the horse is thinking in letters. The horse is capable of activating this philosophical–archetypical–level in me and calling it up in my consciousness, which then produces the image.

I ask Tinnia how I can solve the dilemma of the forking paths. Her answer is again cryptic. She sends me the English word *arbitrary*. Perhaps she is answering in English because I asked her whether I should attend a workshop in England rather than do the training in the U.S.A. and for days I have been looking for flights and hotels. I do not know the word *arbitrary* and look it up in the dictionary. *Arbitrary* is *willkürlich* in German. I notice a shift in my consciousness when I read *willkürlich*. As if my own arbitrariness were withdrawing from me like a ghost which has a searchlight shone at it. At that moment the decision is made. I will not go to England but to Arizona, to attend Linda Kohanov's course. The thoughts that have been circling within me for days have evaporated. I have given up deliberately searching for a solution. I have the feeling the decision was made long before. It was just my mind's cover-up antics and evasive strategies that had held me up. That at least is how it seems to me in retrospect.

I could have plunged into a new contradiction and asked myself whether it was not just one colossal conjuring trick and my consciousness was playing a trick of its own with a horse as an imaginary actor.

Is this question important? Or is something else more important? That I have rediscovered the condition of well-being that horses are such masters of? We cannot control our consciousness, neither can we suspend it, we can only follow it, flow with it. Till the next contradiction comes along, till we are confronted with the next decision, the next step in the process of our individualization.

It can use up a lot of energy undergoing a contradiction. We have only passed the test when we feel certain again. We have to feel certainty in our bodies.

A horse leads you to this certainty.

Horses are looking for 'safety and comfort', says the world-famous horse trainer Pat Parelli. His method aims at linking the goal he wants to achieve with a feeling of well-being. It is this method which is used in behavioural therapy: specific behavioural patterns are linked to positive feelings.

The future of psychology, according to the Californian psychiatrist Stan Grof, lies beyond behavioural therapy. Because none of the existing psychological models provides an answer to the question of what happens in the psyche when a person has spiritual insights, when his consciousness, following an inner dynamic, is transformed and gains access to new layers of perception and insight.

Horses look not only for physical and mental well-being but also for emotional and spiritual harmony. They delight in the interplay of all the elements of the psyche. They themselves are the fifth element. That is where genuine well-being lies.

What contradictions are you involved in at this moment?

Look at your life and write down what either-or situations you are facing. Find a major either-or situation that spans your whole life, perhaps from birth right up to the present point in time. Find a minor either-or situation in your everyday life, today, e.g.: shall I go to the cinema or fill in my tax declaration instead? How does it feel to be faced with a decision which needs to be made? Contradiction is part of life. It

is loaded with tension and therefore strenuous. In films and books it bears a large proportion of the action: will the wealthy millionaire Edward and the prostitute Vivian fall in love or will things just remain business? Will Scarlett O'Hara in *Gone With the Wind* realize in time that she loves Rhett Butler?

Contradictions are nothing negative. We need them for our personal development. We participate in the contradictions of others, including fictional characters, in order to learn and to gather experience.

How to you behave in a contradiction? Do you recognize a pattern in your behaviour? How do you find solutions?

Now is the time to make notes. Do you feel this step physically? Emotionally? Or does the solution only take place in your head? Examine yourself and, if you have the opportunity, seek the advice of a horse. Perhaps it has a totally different answer for you from what you expected.

Step Eight
Failure

The roots of the hero's journey reach back to a time when human feeling was adjusted to the rhythms of nature. Failure, defeat, accidents, death, injuries were not part of a personal system of evaluation as in contemporary culture. As members of an individualized society based on achievement we experience failure as personal guilt, accompanied by the highly unpleasant feeling of remorse. Failure triggers in us the fear of being expelled, of being homeless, helpless and lonely.

Once I was sitting with a group of African friends in Niamey, the capital of the desert state of Niger. One of them had brought along a giraffe carved from wood, as a work of art it was a miserable failure. The animal displayed such a stupid expression that we spent the evening laughing like hyenas about this unspeakable piece of workmanship. The uncharitable comments got cruder and cruder: a shrunken elephant farting, a slimy snotty-nosed antelope, we rolled about hooting with laughter. The meaning of the whole thing was not to insult the 'artist' but to free ourselves from our own fear of failure. The giraffe stood for everything that we ourselves had miserably failed in. We kept laughing until the interest in the giraffe evaporated and we were rid of our fear. You doubtlessly know Troubadix, the lamentably awful singer in the *Asterix* comics. His singing is abominable, nobody in the village likes him, but they all need him so that in contrast they themselves don't look so bad.

There is great pressure to be successful, so we drive fear of failure from our consciousness. In our dreams and in silent moments it attacks us like a hungry animal, hungry for attention.

It is not failure or defeat which are threatening but our fear of them. Failure and defeat are as old as the universe. Nature fails and is defeated: produces crippled trees, mutated plants, blind animals and catastrophes. Nobody would accuse nature of having failed.

Failure is an evaluation produced by measuring a particular action against a predetermined goal. But perhaps the goal made no sense? Perhaps our failures, when we apply different standards, are successes?

A rider who fails in a dressage competition which he has been preparing for months realizes that his horse is not suitable for it and finds fulfilment three years later in a solitary moment in the riding arena when he melds with his horse in complete unity in freestyle dressage.

The special thing about the hero's journey, the reason why it not only has psychological but mythical depth, is revealed in two steps: the present one 'Failure' and the one following: 'Catastrophe'. Without these two steps there is no hero's journey. The heroine sets out with a goal but while she is pursuing this it is brought into question. If the heroine were to pursue her goal consistently, nothing would change for her. Admittedly this is what we all wish for and what the success mongers promise us, but, firstly, that does not coincide with our experience, and, secondly, we do not grow from it. We are not really creative. We are simply following patterns. Large parts of ourselves remain uninvolved. Our emotions remain shallow, our body remains a means to an end, our spirituality slumbers like Sleeping Beauty surrounded by thorny hedges.

When we fail and do not achieve our goal, questions arise, and it is then that we become inventive. Many inventions have come about as a result of failure, of desperation and unsuccessful experiments. Mankind's way is that of learning from experience. What is experience if not a game of failure and success?

How can we get to know ourselves if we do not know how, where, why and when we fail?

When I hand the lead rope to an inexperienced heroine, possibly even one who is afraid of horses, and ask her to lead the horse, her fear of failure is understandably enormous.

Her failure is obvious and immediate, namely, when the horse resists her wish to lead it. In this situation the heroine, as in the sequence of an experiment, can discover how she copes with her fear of failure. Does she freeze? Does she get angry? Does she react with frustration? Does she resort to meaningless actions?

The decisive question is this: is she aware of her fear, her insecurity? When I ask this question and somebody answers that everything is OK and they do not feel any kind of fear, I see as a rule a horse growing more and more nervous, a situation which is escalating. I see a heroine who is heading for danger without noticing it.

It is not fear which is threatening, but how we deal with it. That horses mirror our fear is a truism. When we are learning to ride, we are required to be calm and relaxed when we approach a horse. We are supposed to hide our fear. That is impossible. In contrast to people distorted by civilization, a horse perceives our fear at a highly subtle bodily level, irrespective of whether we are conscious of the fear or not. Therefore if we do not actually succeed in being completely calm, the horse will pick up our fear.

Deliberately wanting to be calm is the exact opposite of really being calm. In the one case we are controlled by our will, in the other our whole being is filled with calmness. An exacting goal, but horses demand nothing less. And not only horses, human beings too. Just like horses, humans pick up our non-verbal signals.

Trying to be calm deliberately means suppressing our fear–and that is precisely what unsettles the horse. It cannot trust a leader who is unaware of his internal chaos. What will this chaotic bundle do when the chips are down? Nothing good, that's for sure.

By forcibly controlling our emotions, we drive ourselves mad. We become slaves of our internalised patterns of feeling. Sooner or later the boiler explodes, something in us says: stop.

To perceive our fear is what is involved in this step of our hero's journey. We may fail and face defeat, but we breathe out and go on. Genuine failure does not last long. What lasts is our attempt to suppress it.

Once we have recognized our fear, our failure, we take in hope with our next breath. Our feelings flow again. Often we then feel joy, success! Our horse, our human counterpart, we ourselves feel confident again.

In equine-supported experiential learning the breakthrough comes at the moment when the heroine says: "I am terrified, I can't make it, the horse is too big, too wild, too …" She has given up resisting her fear—and instantly the horse gives up its resistance to her.

When a horse reacts nervously to a person and it can be discounted that this nervousness comes from a different source (unknown environment, too little exercise, a rope which is too short etc.), the horse says to us: you're not centred, you're not aware.

Does that mean that only a mature personality can have harmonious contact with a horse? We do not have to be Zen Buddhists, enlightened, or horse shamans to enjoy being one with a horse. Unity is nothing more than the moment we become aware of ourselves and the horse responds with trust and affection. This moment is no more significant than when I am lying in my garden sunning myself and I indulge in a daydream. The horse joins me in the river.

If we train this attitude, it rubs off on our lives, our relationships, our horsemanship, and step by step we actually become more conscious human beings. To be a horseman or a horsewoman is not a static condition. We do not have to attain a goal at the end of the journey. It is the condition of being alive, of eternal change. We attain true success when we plunge deeper into the river of life.

At this point I would like to issue a warning. The unity I am describing does not mean you will suddenly become a perfect rider or horse trainer. There is much that is factual or practical to learn about horses and riding. On no account should you approach an unknown horse believing you only need to be slightly high and the

130

horse will kneel before you. Horses are dangerous, they are strong, they are unpredictable if you have not learned to get the measure of them so as to handle them appropriately.

For that reason always be sure of your safety first! Find yourself an experienced horse person to accompany you. Your ability to handle horses will improve when you learn to be more aware–and when you learn at the same time what you need to know, do and practice with these animals. The factual and practical aspects are just as important as awareness. In the end your hard-earned abilities will flourish and you will find *the one thing* described by the legendary American horseman Ray Hunt: "All the technique in the world means nothing without the one thing for which there are no words."

I would like you now to delve a bit deeper with me into the feeling of failure. Up to now you have had a theoretical grounding, the next step is to feel it. In doing so go as far as you can. Your task is not to drown in fear but to feel it and to be consciously aware of it.

What does it feel like to fail? I suggest you have your workbook to hand and look for examples from your life in which you have experienced the feeling of failure. Write them down and go with the feeling of failure and defeat. You can also find examples in which you participated in other people's stories. The newspapers are full of tales of failure.

Comedies thrive on the fear of failing, comic heroes sink deeper and deeper into chaos, into what is indescribably embarrassing, into the whirlpool of failure. I ask you, however, not to evade the feeling by laughing about it but to sustain it. Feelings are valuable information bearers. They stand for the element water, which causes everything to flow. Doing so brings solutions into the light of day which come to mind as realizations, movement or even revelations.

To cleanse your feelings is like cleansing your body. Afterwards we feel refreshed and balanced. We can carry out such cleansing together with horses, but first I'd like to ask you to do it on your own.

I will now delve deeply into the fear of failure. If you wish, you can either follow me or remain an observer. It is my experience of the fear of failure. Yours may look different.

The feeling of failure:

A feeling of great weakness. A place populated by people who are weak, people I love very much, I now feel my love for these people and I see the light that surrounds them. I see a man suffering from a serious illness and I see that he is surrounded by gleaming light. I feel great sadness that I cannot always see this light and that I perceive him as weak although I know he is not weak. Although I know that I am just as weak as he is, that all people are so weak–and gleaming just as brightly. This is my failure. I am shivering, it is cold in this place. In the place of truth it is cold. The place of truth frightens me. I have no protection here. When something external, some external endeavour fails, when I am harshly criticised, I am at this place of weakness together with others who have failed. I am with them, I love them, but I still see it as failure.

In that place I see another man, who is mentally ill. He feels great suffering, he finds no anchor point in the world. He is often in hospital and cannot find work, he is exposed to great animosity, his friends mock him. I want to see him more clearly, I ask for a clearer picture. I see him holding a container and I see that it is the womb of the world, a container from which everything is born. He is holding it in his hands. I see his great wisdom. I feel deep love for him as he holds the world in his hands.

I see my horse, the vulnerable expression in my mare's eyes. She lives in this vulnerability but she does not suffer from it. Her vulnerability teaches me that this is the place of love.

I feel weak, I am shivering, I am very cold. If I want to stay in this place of love, I have to give up many things. Then I will fail in the eyes of the world. And whose are the eyes of the world? My eyes?

I think of a man who is very angry. They have gagged and stifled his power. He bears the burden of the world on his shoulders, that is how strong he is but they are afraid of him, they pelt him with stones, not because he is weak but because he is too strong. I think of Merlin, Linda Kohanov's indomitable stallion of whom Yvonne Monahan writes: "The king appears, we bow before his splendour, his power, his glory. But he shows little mercy for those who do not acknowledge his greatness. He just knows that those who try to master him will become humble."

This is a different kind of failure: the refusal to acknowledge my greatness and the greatness of others. Behind my fear of failure lurks the fear of seeing true greatness.

I first fail with external tasks but if I look more closely, I fail because of my own truth. This failure is bitter and sad. It is love which I have rejected. The greatest miracle that I have ever experienced is that this love nonetheless comes back to me. That this love is always there. That there is no such thing as real failure.

I would like you to select an occurrence or a relationship from your life, in which you have failed and go on a journey into the heart of this failure. My journey was just an example. Free yourself from it. You will perhaps experience something quite different. Stay with it, stay with your feelings and write down what you feel without thinking about it. Do not read it through to start with. Do not try to correct it. Leave it just as it is.

Horses are gentle and so are we. But there is a cocoon around us so impenetrable that we no longer perceive our gentleness. We seek refuge with horses to be reminded of this.

I want to be as gentle as horses, free of cravings which make me feel small, of ambition, of the need to be admired. I want to be beautiful, complete. Not because I want to show off with money, fame, a title, honours but because I am already complete.

I have become allergic to the addictive need for success and greatness. I no longer like it in myself nor in other people. I am thin-skinned, I keep away from this energy. I am unfair, but in this phase I have to be. Someday I will grow a second skin which is not so much tough as penetrable. Till then it is my job to make sure the old, tough skin does not come back.

I have to avoid what triggers the old reflexes in me, like an alcoholic for whom chocolates are a danger. My channels are so wide open that I absorb everything. I find it hard to differentiate between what is good for me and what is not. I have given up making judgements. I am raw and vulnerable. I am rowing through fog and have no compass. Only a vague idea, a few insights. Everything is at stake.

I do not know how long this process will take, whether I will survive it or break it off prematurely, whether I will be able to keep my daily life intact or am heading for a catastrophe. Now and again I relapse into the addiction to control everything, to dominate my life and myself.

I can no longer bear to listen to certain kinds of music, read particular books, watch particular films, no longer tolerate the presence of certain people. I seek the company of people who are weak. I am infatuated with showing them my love.

But I am not only weak. At the same time I am strong. I experience joy as never before. I am inspired. I am amazed, I laugh, I celebrate. I seek the company of people who are strong, who do not hide their strength. True weakness and true strength show us clearly that our life task consists of freeing ourselves from external pressures and to awaken to our gentle and strong horse-self. Failures are gateways to love.

I wish for a culture of vulnerability. Vulnerability should not be what we avoid at all costs. Because vulnerability is the essence of growth and creativity and love. Without vulnerability we are condemned to stagnation. I wish for a culture of strength, a culture of true power, greatness and beauty.

Horses embody both: strength and vulnerability. In their fear of a flapping piece of plastic we find our own fear of unpredictable, every-day things. In the proud posturing which they present to their fellow creatures we find our own beauty, our pride, our moments of triumph.

We have learnt that we have to dominate horses, that horses organize their community strictly hierarchically and that we have to be the alpha animal to win their trust.

What does dominance mean?

Most problems between horse and rider, so we are told, have their roots in an unresolved balance of power. We are told that we fail because we have insufficient leadership qualities. The same applies to our failure in the human world: too little bite, too little self-assertion, ambition, power.

In his book *Die Wahrheit über Pferdeflüsterer* (The Truth About Horse Whisperers), which in English is more aptly called *The Horse Breakers*, Clive Richardson has gathered examples of people who subjugated horses, wrapped ropes around their legs and bodies to drag them down. Horses were made pliable by being forced to stand still for days. Even a straightjacket for horses was invented, a leather belt which was buckled under its belly and around its front and back legs.

A subjugated horse, one whose will has been broken, does not trust people. It always remains uncooperative, it will often bite, become malicious or it will obey without conviction and has to be constantly driven on, will injure itself and fall ill. No different, in fact, from a human being exposed to suppression and the abuse of power.

This kind of dominance is no solution. What then is meant by dominance?

Richardson quotes the method of the English horse-tamer John Rarey from the end of the nineteenth century: "His long experience makes it possible for him to predict the horse's behaviour in critical

136

moments from sudden muscle tension alone, and so just about avoid being kicked." That horse-tamer possessed the gift of watchfulness. He was so closely connected to the horses that their bodily tensions were transmitted to his body without passing through mental channels. It is impossible for a human being to dominate a horse physically, simply because it weighs ten times more and has ten times more muscle power. Dominance has to be transmitted via different channels. Willpower is not enough.

It does not interest a horse whether I *want* to lead it but whether I *can* lead it. I can lead it if I possess both awareness and conviction. When my will and my being are unified. Then my horse's will and being are unified, too. That reminds me of a conversation I recently had with the former head of a psychiatric department. Talking about his work with excitable psychiatric patients he revealed this to me: "My therapeutic tool was my own body. I knew when the patient was losing his self-control and I had to change my therapeutic strategy. I felt it through tension in my back."

A psychotherapist told me about a patient of hers who always brought her dog along to her therapy sessions. "I knew the therapy was successful when the dog laid its head in the patient's lap. Because the dog made no mistakes."

That is the level on which we gain the horses' trust. In a herd of horses the lead animals are mostly old, experienced mares. Animals which are not concerned with showing off their power but with harmony and safety in their herd.

If we want to *lead* horses, we have to empathize with them, enter into an exchange with them. Then we enter into the flow of movement, of impulses, of joy, of fear, of attentiveness, of decisiveness. That is the secret of *dominance*.

137

It is a great and a small art. Anyone can do it. Even if he has never had anything to do with horses, he will succeed in most cases in establishing the connection. No matter whether he is strong or weak, vigorous or fragile, man or woman. It is that communication between creatures described by Andreas Weber: "For centuries science has been explaining to us that our enjoyment of other living creatures is a sentimental illusion. Such a point of view ignores a deep human emotion. Contemporary researchers are discovering that it is precisely our feelings which lead to the fundamental questions of modern science. This message is of course so radical that until now it has not always been understood. It means nothing other than that the world is not an alien place ... We share it with countless other organisms who feel just as much as we do."

Go back once more to that place of failure and to the people there. What relationship do you have with these people? Do you dominate them? Do they dominate you? Or are you equals? What causes your relationships to fail? Are you caught in a vicious circle of submissive games? Have you become addicted to a relationship as you would to a drug? Or are you free and strong?

What relationship do you have with your horse? With horses in general. What makes your relationships with horses fail? Are you and your horse caught in a vicious circle of dominance and resistance? Do you seek results and find failure? What really causes you to fail?

Can you see your relationships as they are and change them from there? Can you feel the strength which is hidden behind your failure?

Step Nine
Catastrophe

I would like to run away, far, far away. There seems to be no place for me in this world. I am alone, nobody understands me, nobody sees things the way I do. I weep for the flayed creature who has been made to suffer so much—and if I have the courage to be honest, I cry for myself. The animals do not need my tears. This is a further lesson they have taught me. I do not even have an excuse to weep about the poor horses who are thought to be weaker. These weak ones reject my sympathy stubbornly—it is thrown back in my face. It is me who is the weak one. It is hard to look this truth in the eye.

I have lived my life avoiding this weakness. There are hardly any ways I do *not* know of avoiding and denying my weakness. My repertoire of remaining aloof is impressive.

Now that I come to see through it, I am shocked. I can no longer play these games, wear these masks. There is virtually nothing left of me. I can hardly stand upright any more. "When people are alienated from nature, their hearts become hard," says Chief Luther Standing Bear of the Lakota Sioux. I can feel this hardness in myself. Suddenly right in the middle of a sentence I am struck dumb, I pause in mid-gesture. How could I have allowed this hardness to arise? Have I trained for it? Modelled myself on it?

I see people through different eyes. I see beyond the personality that civilization has foisted on them. I see members of a tribe, children in whom nature is still alive. I see the wounds that civilization has inflicted on them. I see the grotesque masks they have put on–to protect themselves. I understand them–I love them like my brothers and sisters. They are horses. Members of a herd.

"Horses are unshaken in their hope that humanity will wake up," said Kate Solisti-Mattelon in her book *Conversations With Horses*.

Waking up hurts. I feel incapable of taking any step because I have lost my direction. I tremble with fear of the unknown, I am doubled up with the pain. Pain and cold force me to stay in my body. The body is the only safe place, say the horses. The fear forces you to stay awake.

How can I go on functioning in the world?

There is a huge STOP sign in me!

"Although I have won prestigious prizes for my work and had the feeling I was riding the crest of the wave, I could not ignore the growing emptiness and the feeling that my life had gone out of balance," writes the photographer Tony Stromberg in the preface to his book of photographs *Spirit Horses*. "When I gave more space to the whispering beneath the surface, my need for external recognition vanished."

Like my fellow human beings I am starving for recognition. There can never be enough: prizes, salary increases, marks, cups, hymns of praise, flattery. Is it that we are cut off from nature that creates this insatiable hunger in us? We do not understand what the whites want, said the Native Americans when they saw the whites slaughtering bison, fencing off land and rooting through the earth for gold.

As the ice melts, great distrust of myself emerges. As an artist I saw myself as the personification of a collective feeling. Now I experience how shaky this collective is. I have to steer for the river bank to avoid sinking. I have just about made it. A survivor!

In a nightmare I lose my connection to the group. Horses are waiting for me. They are now my companions, my home.

There is a moving scene in the documentary film *Cloud* made by Ginger Kathrens, who has been observing wild horses for many years. The stallion, Cloud, fights his rivals for his own herd, his own mares, and fails, until he notices that as the herd moves on one of the mares stays behind with her new-born foal. He takes this mare and her foal under his wing. Cloud thus finds his herd not by using force but by an act of empathy.

Susan Chernak McElroy writes in *Animals As Teachers And Healers*: "In their innocence and wisdom, in their connection to the earth and its primeval rhythms, animals show us a way back to a home they have never left."

The catastrophe in the hero's journey is the point at which the hero loses everything. Not only has he failed but he has suffered injury to his soul. His old system of values breaks down. There are losses, real deaths, or death to parts of his own self. The loss is not just imagined fear, it is real. It has consequences. A relationship, a marriage has broken down. A job is lost, a horse has died. We have to toil on through pain, fear and insecurity.

Our world turns out to be an illusion, the great lover a deceiver, the well-paid job a nightmare, the business partner bankrupt. Our horse, our superbly behaved favourite, starts to buck and bolt. What do we do at our wit's end?

The way is not complete until we have gone through fire. No matter how successful we are, sooner or later a crisis awaits us, a break, a separation. For a time we may manage to keep the old and the new lives together, but sooner or later we have to decide, our inner life decides. Sooner or later we wake up.

Authentic life demands sacrifices. We are not used to making sacrifices. Sacrifice in our self-assertive culture is taboo. In ancient cultures sacrifice is seen as an honour. It is embedded in rituals, it harbours necessity and brings new strength, connection to the gods. If we follow our heart's desire, we reach the point where a sacrifice is demanded of us.

Do you remember the goal you set for yourself in step four of the journey? Have you reached it? Have you lost sight of it on the way? Have you failed at it? I suggest you to go through your notes and ask yourself what has happened to your goal.

My goal was to complete this book. My challenge consisted not in mastering the way for others but in becoming master of myself. I have almost finished writing the book. I do not feel like a master. At the very most I am on my way.

What was your challenge? What attitude, what motif, what mantra was supposed to accompany you on your way? And what has actually happened on your journey? Is there a point that hurts? A shadow you cannot jump over?

If we follow our heart's desire, we reach a point where nothing works any more. We can no longer stay in an unloving relationship, no longer carry out work which oppresses our soul. We can no longer lock our horse up in a box. We break with friends, employers, business ideas and training courses. We give up our flats, towns, countries, societies, clubs, hobbies, family members or even our horses.

And when we have done with all this separation business, we go to the stable or stand at a pasture fence. The horses are still there. We mean something to the horses, we are recognized and appreciated, not for our huge egos, though, but for our sheer existence. And we have never needed anything else. We had to make sacrifices to finally come closer to ourselves.

Catastrophe is the cleansing fire.

Your task: light a torch. And go through your life. Find all that is dried up and will burn easily. Find all that is unclear, all that is vague, shaky, everything that has long been shrivel-

ling up. And set fire to it! Fan the great fire. Throw in your sacrificial objects to the goddess.

When you have finished, go into the stable and do something simple with your horse. Something QUITE simple. Without ambition, without glancing sideways at the goal. Breathe with your horse. And never forget that moment ever again.

What is art? What is writing? What have I been doing for twenty years? What do I do with my fellow human beings, with my children, with myself? Tony Stromberg, famous player in the advertising photography game, writes: "I have finally left the world of false security and business culture to follow a path which has *nurtured* the living world and spirituality, rather than negating them." Contact with horses and the lost values they embody awoke in Tony Stromberg the "vague hope of a new faith, that I could do something I loved and that nourished me spiritually." Is it madness for a man who has worked creatively his whole life long to feel like this? That for him it is only now that true creativity is beginning?

Anna Halprin, the founder of creative arts therapy, found herself in a similar crisis after contracting cancer. "Modern dance at that time involved dancing to themes, ... Greek mythology or to music and other abstract things. I was no longer interested in the abstract. I began to explore ways in which I could dance to themes that concerned real life–my life ... you must expose yourself to what is ... it can be challenging, dark and uncomfortable. But readiness to use the artistic process to overcome blockages–that is creative."

Is it a question of creating or of being? Two years ago I stuck an affirmation to the top edge of my monitor: I am a medium. I will now remove it. *I am a medium.* When am I going to start being myself? And cease being a controlling power, one which forces things, or spinelessly receives and accepts–my children, my horse, my fellow human beings, myself? To lose power is one part of catastrophe.

The other part is finally to acknowledge our strength. Is *this* catastrophe possibly worse? "Our greatest fear", says the poet Marianne Williamson, "is not that we are insufficient, weak and mediocre, but that our greatness shatters every boundary."

Are we heroines more than anything else? And does the catastrophe consist in allowing ourselves to be strong, to love, to see, to make the connection? That we know enumerable 'yes, buts'? That we wait for permission to be creative and individual? That we cannot cope with anybody criticizing or rejecting us? That we submissively take back our truth? To do whom a favour? Certainly not ourselves, nor anybody else, for that matter, because aren't other people the same scaredy-cats we are? What do other people need us for if not to go ahead of us and say: here, in this place, we'll be fine. The same way as horses always and indefatigably give us to understand.

The great catastrophe at this stage of the hero's journey is to know and to have found out where our heart lies. If we cannot live in this place, we are condemned to damnation.

Lovers whose love is not returned–can they nonetheless live in the place of their love? Yes. The seeker who does not find–can he live in the place of his search? The artist who does not discover a form of expression–can she live in that place of powerlessness?

145

The rider whose horse refuses—can she accept the place of her helplessness? The suicide case who cannot gain access to her world—can she inhabit the place of her loneliness without taking her life? Until life returns? Can all these heroes bear life without fleeing into illusion? Can they bear the pain until something new is born?

On my way home to Germany from the Epona Center in Arizona I had a fairly long stay in Atlanta, at one of the world's largest airports where 200,000 people arrive and depart daily. Somebody had had the idea of installing a grand piano right in the midst of the thousands streaming by. An elderly, unkempt pianist was playing Schumann improvisations. I burst into tears. I was ashamed of my lack of self- control. But I saw no one at all looking down on me as I had feared, instead I saw that like me, they too were feeling fear, pain and weakness and the beauty of the music. The airport terminal presented a picture of human communality. Hectic, nervous people lost in self-forgetfulness, and in their midst the beauty of their souls, embodied in the musician's playing. Real disaster stems from our inability to live our true selves. That something holds us back from it. That this something which we are is so difficult to find. We discover it in moments of finality, such as those shortly before the Titanic sinks into the freezing Arctic depths, impressively depicted in the film *Titanic*. The true essence of those aboard is revealed in these moments before annihilation. Some dance, others go looting, the captain is turned to stone.

A single trauma—or a long process of adaptation—has distorted access to our centre. We must return to the source, that seam, through which concrete comes pouring into our lives. If we go to horses, we can ask them how we may find redress.

Horses say there is no guilt. That thing, that person you feel guilty about is the gateway to your liberation. Your pain is the bridge to love. Your fear, your fury are your saviours.

Everybody has such a gate, such a bridge, such saviours.

For Shelley Rosenberg, dressage rider and ranch manager at the Epona Center, the way began at the age of two, when she was abused by her grandfather, and from then on could only bear the company of horses. She has written a book about her journey, which ultimately brought her closer to horses than she could have ever thought possible. Her book gives others the courage to share their stories, not stories of success, but authentic stories.

Whatever you do, no matter how good or diligent you are, however much you love, worry or struggle, you will never succeed in being anything other than you yourself.

This is the essence of catastrophe. You are not worth it, you do not deserve it. You will never attain wisdom. You will never establish a bond with horses, you will not hear their voices, nor feel their love, their pain. Do you believe this?

Do you know all those spells you have cast on yourself?

I am not ...

I will never ...

I am not allowed to ...

I cannot ...

I am too ...

I have no right to ...

Never ...

Complete your list. Write down everything that comes to mind. Everything that prevents you from being yourself–at this very moment. And then curse. Hurl anathema at this rubbish. Put a spell on it. Do what you enjoy doing and let your hair down. Let that be the end of it, once and for all.

What do you do if someone tries to palm you off with junk at an excessive price?–You don't buy it.

What do you do when you discover that items you have bought are damaged?–Demand your money back.

What do you do when the love you have been promised turns out to be inflated nothing?–You say good-bye for ever.

The spells lurking in your head are junk that was palmed off on you. You can give it back. That is not you. You have a right to live. Even a right to be happy. Don't you think so? Even a right to be divine.

The sensitive horse becomes leader of the herd because it recognizes dangers before others do. While the self-satisfied bask in their strength, the watchful horse sounds the call for flight. Do not let this predator get any closer!

What predators are threatening your life? Ask your body. Ask your horse. Name your predator and feel its energy. The sensitive animal by your side will tell you how far to run. Not a step too few nor a step too many. Horses use their energy economically.

Get yourself to safety.

At the centre of the storm, where are the signposts? Can you keep a clear head and ask the way from someone who knows? Can you find the information that will show you the way out of the storm?

Can you feel something is moving, even if, from the outside, it seems to be standing still? Is it inherent in your journey that you no longer do certain things before you begin anything?

Can you find true connection to yourself in the midst of catastrophe? Can you find the gateway? Is it music? Is it silent companionship with your horse? Is it concern for a person you love? Or is it something else?

Sometimes I come across people who feel sorry for me because I have a horse: so much time, so much work, so much money. Often it is the very things that worry us, that are strenuous, that make us desperate, which can become the gateway. It is just that we are unaware that 'the Way is not the difficulty, difficulty is the Way'.

Recently I asked my farrier whether he had noticed that people were selling their horses because of the economic crisis. They would rather, he said, do without everything else. 70% to 80% of horse owners are women. Do we need catastrophes because they are the way to our liberation?

My answer is: yes.

Step Ten
Climax

A leap of faith, say the Hollywood script writers, is part of the climax. A leap into jeopardy, blind trust. The moment when darkness becomes light. That is the climax of the hero's journey. It is the moment when the demon flees because his name has been spoken aloud. The moment when we let go. Whether it is a small step or a large one makes no difference.

Ingrid had been invited to demonstrate her work based on natural horsemanship to a series of interested people. It was to be her first appearance in public. She was nervous and soon realized that the horse allocated to her, the Appaloosa mare Mariah, was not going to cooperate and that the whole performance would degenerate into tortured chaos. Instead of pretending she had everything under control, she turned to the audience and said: "I'm sorry but the horse is not ready and neither am I. I can't show you anything."

Ingrid felt miserable. To her surprise, though, rather than being booed, she gained approval. The audience was impressed that someone should have the courage to accept and articulate what was obvious, instead of pretending. Each one of them knew such moments with a horse and the concomitant feeling of helplessness. The audience understood that this was the actual message. The mare, which had been so difficult the whole time, turned to Ingrid and put her head on her shoulder.

The climax is the moment when the horse comes to us, the moment of connection. When the horse is there, it is really there. Not half there, or a quarter there, but there completely. To begin with perhaps we hardly even realize this. It hardly feels any different than it normally does. Why does the horse suddenly cooperate? Why does it come up to me and breathe in my ear? It is hard to believe that that can have anything to do with me. We consider it to be a whim on the part of the horse. And our horse has already disappeared again. That in its turn we take as confirmation that it cannot have been anything special. But the horse came because of us, and it went because of us.

The difficulty in dealing with horses is that their perception is too subtle for our blunted senses. We do not hear nature's message because it is on the borderline of our ability to perceive. If we refine our perception a new world opens up before us.

Everyone who experiences this is speechless with astonishment.

At the climax of the heroic journey you perhaps expect something magnificent, a message that will transform your life. A magic formula or a miracle. But what happens is something quiet, something barely perceptible.

What is happening at this very moment in your life? What are you sad about, impatient, happy, excited, annoyed, hurt? The moment, the feeling that you have at this very moment, is your gateway. No matter how you are feeling just now, this is your point of departure. Here you will find the answer. If you do not find it here, you will not find it anywhere else either.

Today I have to fight the feeling that everything is going too slowly, that I cannot reach, realize my goals, my dreams, my wishes fast enough. That reminds me of a painful time when I was seventeen and unhappy in love. For hours I sat at the window waiting for the boy I loved to go past on his motorbike. He did not come but nevertheless I could not give up waiting. Climax.

Instead of providing you with a magic spell to fulfil your wishes, to take along with you on your journey, I ask you to invite into your life that moment of waiting, of expectation, of wishing and hoping. While I was waiting for that unhappy love, I became acquainted with the essence of waiting, I gained wisdom that has accompanied me throughout my life.

While we are waiting, we get the feeling that nothing is happening. We are not aware that something is always happening. Being under the constant pressure of time and the lure of success, we find it hard to believe that waiting is supposed to be movement. In nature there are many periods of waiting and transition in which nothing appears to be happening. Suddenly a caterpillar becomes a butterfly, trees suddenly blossom. We instant-happiness people constantly try to banish waiting from our lives and in doing so cut away life at the same time.

Life always moves. Stop staring at it. If you became aware of how alive your life really is, it would blow your mind. What then is the climax of the heroic journey with horses?

If we lived in a different age, I would conjure up for you *climax* in the form of a magnificent firework display of the senses and of enlightenment. But we already have enough of that. We are constantly surrounded and pressured by dazzling climaxes.

The breakthrough to horses takes places when the horses believe us. New every time. The most difficult thing in the art of acting is sitting silently on a chair in such a way that a theatre full of people hold their breath. An art that only a completely authentic actor can master. It is an art of letting go, the being of not-being.

The connection to horses is something invisible. The climax on the heroic journey with horses is an anti-climax. It is the silent flowing back and forth of energy. Question and answer. Flowing *with* things. Revelation, forgetting. This is why we are drawn back to the stable again and again. Because something tells us that everything revolves round this. That every failure, every catastrophe leads to this. The silent connection to horses seems like Nothing, but it is Everything. We speak the language of nature and nature answers.

We have become members of a tribe. We have found the connection to our ancestors. We see the world with our inner eye. Suddenly we know for sure. Suddenly we love forever. Suddenly our life is no longer a show. Suddenly we are meaningful. Suddenly we have a task. Suddenly decisions become easy. Suddenly our wounds heal. Suddenly we achieve our goals.

The journey is not over. We journey on, with every breath. Out beyond our death.

I am talking about immortality. It is remarkable that our ancestors, the Celts, stood out because of their faith in immortality. Perhaps my long involvement with the Celts led me to see that the immortality of all living things is self-evident, and to see the belief that man's soul disappears after death is simply absurd.

Feel free to believe whatever you see as right, even if it does not coincide with what you have learned about religion. If we have no freedom in spiritual affairs, what freedom do we have at all?

What do you believe in? What is your own completely private belief, valid only for you? Belief in the immortality of the soul, in God, in karma, reincarnation, beauty, the belief that in an earlier life you were a goddess, a witch, a priestess? In Atlantis or in a circle of wise men, who have sent you down to earth to complete a task? Are you an atheist, a nihilist, an existialist or do you prefer not to believe in anything that has a name? You are free to believe in what gives you courage and fulfilment. Write your vision down, or paint it, or find something in nature that reflects your belief.

While I was working on a book about the Celts, I had a vision that took me back to their time. What happened was so real that I had the feeling I had gone down a time-channel directly to that time, or at least to a time-field stored in some collective mind. I could talk to people from that time, question them. Their answers were more convincing than anything I had ever read about them. Since then I have known that life is unending and that we are linked to our ancestors.

Two years after this vision I stumbled across a stone slab on a busy square in the town we had meanwhile moved to. I was struck by Celtic symbols carved into the slab. Amongst other things a figure with a three-cornered hat like the one I had seen in my vision. On the back of the stone it said: "From 400 B.C. to 100 A.D. the Celts lived on both sides of present-day Stuttgart Road." Just where my husband and I had recently bought a house. Unintentionally I live on what was once Celtic ground.

I share the Celts' belief in immortality. I am indebted to them for many insights, for love and understanding. Needless to say, the Celts were a great equestrian people, horses permeate their mythology and symbolism. The book deals with the Celtic horse goddess Epona. The research for it took me to Linda Kohanov's Epona Center—and to a new life in which I not only write about the Celts but also live inspired by their ideas.

The belief in immortality contains a message which has special significance for those people who believe they do not have enough time to do everything they have planned. That means: virtually all of us.

I have learned from the Celts that there is no such thing as too little time. Nor too much time. Each of us has as much time as we need.

A breakthrough in horse training sometimes comes quickly, sometimes it takes months. A horse's learning process follows its natural rhythm, its abilities, its growth.

When we learn to no longer control time and to recognize movement in stillness, we experience a genuine climax. It can be big and explosive like a life-changing event, or as small as a breath in which we overcome our separation.

I know it takes a lot to resist the inner feeling of being driven. It requires nothing less than the very opposite of what is demanded of us right round the clock. Be patient with yourself. Many climaxes are waiting for you.

"On the way, during my indefatigable search, horses taught me the unbounded movement of every living thing. Each time I felt a breakthrough in my learning process I opened the door and my horse said to me: and about time, too! I've been waiting for you. A few weeks later I experienced a new breakthrough. I opened the door and my horse was there again. Up to now I have never experienced any limitation, apart from my own." Dominique Barbier

The steppes are open on all sides. At the top of a rise, where our gaze can sweep unhindered across the landscape, we inhale the aromatic fragrance of herbs. The tribes from the steppes, the Mongolians, the Huns forced great empires to their knees. But when they penetrated into civilization, they perished. Their horses could no longer find food. Their natural courage shrivelled to the level of pleasure seeking.

Can you find the steppe within yourself? The place of courage? The place where your view is unrestricted and you can survey the whole landscape? That elevated point from which you find insight, security, wisdom? What do you see there?

It is gratifying to watch how people change by experiencing the creative process, by their communion with horses. Even if the journey goes wrong, if the horse gets sick or dies, if a person has to go through fire. When Christina first went to Wyoming to take a holiday on a ranch, she fell in love with the silent prairie. It seemed impossible that she would be able to live there permanently. She had her own two horses to take care of and a job. Today Christina spends most of the year there. She works on the ranch, her old firm has agreed that she can work in Switzerland for the winter months. She has found someone to look after her horses lovingly. Everything falls into place if your wish is strong enough. Christina has found happiness.

The realization of apparently impossible dreams has become much more likely now that the whole world is on the move. Even people's old dream of being one with horses is progressing. If that is not a climax ...

Step Eleven
Conclusion

The heroine has changed noticeably, she has matured personally, has integrated her weakness and thus become a rounded personality. This provides a definition for the last step of the heroic journey.

What has the end of your journey brought you to? Do you remember your departure? Your weakness? Your strength? How have these two qualities developed? How did they influence your route?

Were you able to combine these two qualities, make them a part of your personality? Can you see weakness in your strength and strength in your weakness? Can you see how

they both belong together? Have you found your centre? Your name? Look for an image or an object that stands for the conclusion of your journey. A fare-well gift.

What have I arrived at with my strength–which is seeing what is essential–and my weakness–which is absorbing too much that is unfiltered? They have brought forth a book that lurches from order to dissolution–or blends both into one.

Above all it is a personal book. In my lifelong career as an author I had never written about myself. I have now broken that taboo. Not because I feel so great and important. Something different has happened. Lynne Silver, a meditation teacher from Texas, one of our trainers at the Epona Center, describes it like this: "What concerns us here is a different kind of creativity. You are not the one who produces something creative but you yourself are created anew."

What place have you reached that you have never been to before? What taboo, what inner no-go area have you transcended?

The last stage in a film is sometimes an ironic comment, as in *Pretty Woman* where a passer-by says: "This is Hollywood. Here dreams come true."

In the previous step, 'climax', we were standing on the hill and looking at the church tower from above, seeing structure, order, pattern. We saw how everything is linked together and forms a larger picture. With this last step we say farewell. The image becomes a memory. It congeals into a many-layered symbol, an image, an epigram, a snapshot.

I remember my fear of being an outsider. The fear is still there. It has even become worse because with this book I am adopting a vulnerable position. But if I look closely, it does not really frighten me. For I now know that I am not alone. Not only have I got to know many people who feel the way I do—I also have animals on my side. A dream reflected my new confidence in an image which I deliberately recall when my fear returns. I was sitting on a city park bench amongst countless other people—and slept like an innocent child.

To sound a concluding note, I would like to give you something to take with you, something about animal communication, a clue to how one can learn to talk to animals. Everybody is intuitive. It belongs to our survival strategies. Everybody has dreams, inspiration, intuitions, visions. Everybody can feel what another being feels. A baby possesses the whole spectrum of feeling without having learned it from anybody. This was shown by the investigations of the American cognition researchers Andrew Meltzoff and Keith Moore in the mid-nineties. We need no other abilities than what the baby already has.

On the subject of babies' attempts to communicate with their environment Andreas Weber writes: "Babies obviously know that their mother's body is equipped with the very same inwardness."

The same goes for animal communication.

We do not need to learn animal communication. We only have to remove the blockages that prevent us from hearing, seeing, feeling what we already perceive anyway. Animals talk to us via intuitive channels. Everyone hears them differently. Some hear words, some see pictures, others perceive smells, colours, sounds, music or bodily tension.

In all the workshops in which I have practiced intuition, I have never experienced anybody who was incapable of receiving these subtle messages. This ability improves with practice. Concentration is a prerequisite. Everyone has his own rituals for that. A ritual to refine perception can be just as easy as hearing the sound a needle makes when it falls to the ground.

Take a sheet of paper, draw something that comes to mind and study the drawing. When you concentrate on it for a while, it will begin to talk to you. If you ask an animal to help you read the drawing, you will get interesting information. This is just one example amongst many. Find your own exercises, your own channels. Pay attention to your dreams.

Gradually animals will grant you access to that other reality. Then it will become easier and easier. The animals will lead you. Your authentic self will lead you.

A dream of mine about my cats, Momo and Mia, comes to mind: Mia placed Momo's torn-off head at my feet. I dreamt this the night after the massacre in the school in Winnenden. Head and body are separated, that is our society's spiritual condition.

My 14-year-old daughter recently received a message from her horse with a similar meaning. "Carry your thoughts." This sentence suddenly popped up in Lea's head as she was leading the mare to the stable, it means: give your thoughts a body. The next night she dreamt that she was a doctor and had found the right medicine for a patient. Chiron, that powerful archetype of the healer, revealed himself in Lea's experience and in her dream, as if he wanted to reinforce her experience. Chiron was the Greek inventor of medicine, a creature with the torso of a man on the body of a horse. Healing occurs when we place the head back on the body. When we combine our human head with the animal's body.

We need whole human beings if we want to find solutions for the future. The violent separation of head and body is the striking image which finally became visible for me when I looked from a higher viewpoint.

"All my life people have been telling me that my intuition is insane and bad," a seminar participant recently told me. "And if not bad, then useless."

I dedicate this book to all those who have the courage and the heart to use their intuitive potential and thereby make an important contribution to our society. On the way from babyhood to adulthood we learn to cut off our heads, we do not learn healing.

Animals remind us of our bodies. They tell us that it is divided just as my cats did in the dream. Animals say this without reproach, they just convey a sober observation.

They give us pleasant dreams with the same naturalness, like my recent dream of riding my mare with neither saddle nor bridle through a busy village, my head on my body and my body at one with my horse.

Reuniting head and body is the ritual that many perform when they go to the stable. When they set off they are divided, when they return they are whole. Something happens to us when we connect with these animals, with their large communicative bodies, their sensitive hearts and soft eyes.

We are in love with the culture of the American Indians. Can we also be our own Indians? From our Indian ancestors, the Celts, we can learn that this consciousness is also alive in our history.

"The Celts speak in short, enigmatic sentences which often have a double meaning: one in the foreground and one which reveals itself in the mind," the Greek historian Diodorus reports. The Celts inhabited both worlds, this world and the world beyond. Can we rediscover their consciousness in our time?

It is not easy to remember this, but our survival could depend on it.

Go out into life, hero.

Fly on the wings of horses ...

Safety Measures

The method of working with horses described in this book is meant to refine our perception, so that we can make contact with these naturally more sensitive creatures.

As in all contact with horses, however, our highest priority is safety for both human and animal.

Please, therefore, do not carry out any experiments outside a protected environment. The method is not magical and if it does seem to work miracles that is because of more conscious awareness, and a more authentic relationship of the human being with himself and with his horse. This method, even if it sometimes produces tremendous breakthroughs, consists of many small steps. If you are attentive, you will see for yourself what assumptions you can make about your own and your horse's limits. If you are uncertain, please seek advice from someone who has experience handling horses.

The horse you are working with must be sufficiently trained to feel at ease around people, to feel relaxed and inwardly balanced.

A horse does not need special training to be used in equine-facilitated learning because this sort of intuitive communication is second-nature to him. There are, however, horses which do not enjoy it, horse which generally dislike contact with humans. On the other hand through this work horses can develop, can become livelier, more self-confident.

A prerequisite for this interaction is a protected environment in which neither human nor horse is under threat.

Summary of Tasks

The Eleven Steps
on the Hero's Journey

Step One
Who am I?

• Who am I, now, today, at this moment? Give a spontaneous answer. Write it down, until you perceive it physically.

• What is your strength? Find a particular, personal answer. Ask for a feeling.

• What is your experience with horses up till now? How did it begin? Where has it led you? Where do you stand today? What questions do you have for horses and for yourself?

• Can you describe your weakness? A lifelong weakness? A weakness of recent weeks/months, a weakness at this moment? Do you recognize any connection between your answers, a common theme?

Step Two
The Call to Adventure

• Find two or three events in your life which represent a call to adventure and write them down. Ask yourself what has become of them. What meaning has crystallized out from the subsequent developments?

• Is there a call which is related to horses?

• Can you observe the call to adventure in other people's lives? In films and novels?

Step Three
The Wound

• Your wound is the key to the heart of the creature. Do not accept any hint of falseness. Welcome your tears. Be gentle with your fear. Choose your words carefully as they flow from your soul.

• What wounds have horses inflicted on you?

• Can you recognize the message behind your wounds? To which real feeling have they led you?

• Can you see yourself? The whole picture? If you wish, make a drawing.

• Have you felt that moment when the horse leant towards you because you were completely present?

Step Four
The Goal

• What is your goal with horses? Write down what first comes to mind.

• What is your relationship with horses? What dreams do you have about them?

• Decide on a goal. Keep the description of your goal simple and decisive.

• Draw an oracle card or open a philosophical or spiritual book at random. What does the card or passage tell you about the symbol or mantra which accompanies you in realizing your goal?

• Draw up a contract with yourself which contains your goal and your mantra giving date and signature.

Step Five
Connection

• Think of a relationship which is important to you at the moment. What feelings does it arouse in you? What needs does it evoke? What are you lacking? What makes you happy? Then put yourself in the other person's position. How does he or she feel? What do they need? What are they lacking? What makes them happy?

• What stories can you tell about horses? In these stories you will find yourself again. Write the story down and find in it the message which is aimed at you.

• Take your horse into a round pen or another fenced-off area. Concentrate on the relationship which is important to you right now, sense where there is tension in your body. Then ask this place in your body for a feeling. Turn to your horse and go back into your body. Try to establish contact with your horse. Observe your horse's reaction. Observe how your feelings change and how your horse reacts to that. Continue the process until you feel that it has reached a conclusion. You will know that when the tension is resolved. Write down what you have experienced.

• Try to work through at least two such emotional processes on different subjects. The second process does not necessarily have to be a relationship problem. The important thing is to find the connection.

Step Six
The Heart of the Creature

• Have you found the place of gentleness in yourself and gained an idea of what effects that can have on your life?

• Have you experienced how weak you are without your ego's dreams of omnipotence?

• Have you experienced how your horse leans towards you when you are really present, when you are laughing or crying?

• Is there some meditative activity which you repeat regularly and can you see a development there? Is there a breakthrough?

• Have you found a power which comes from both without and from within yourself?

• Have you found your own creature heart independent of other people's routes?

• What stage have you reached on your journey? What have you found there? On this step of the heroic journey it is up to you how you express your experience, in words, images, actions. But do express it. So you can remember it.

Step Seven
Contradiction

• Set up a ritual to find a second name for you, for your invisible self. Or go to your horse and ask it for one.

• Look at your life and write down the contradictions in which you are involved. Find a major either-or situation which spans your whole life. Find a minor either-or situation in your everyday life, today.

• How does it feel to be involved in a decision process which is waiting for solution? How to you behave in a contradiction? Do you recognize a pattern in your behaviour?

• How do you find solutions? How does the solution feel? Is it a real solution or does it only take place in your head?

• Examine yourself and if you have the chance, seek advice from a horse. Perhaps it has a completely different answer for you.

Step Eight
Failure

• Look for examples from your life in which you have experienced the feeling of failure. You can also find examples in which you have shared the feelings in other people's stories.

• Select an occurrence and go on a journey to the heart of your failure. Stay with it and with your feelings and write down what you feel without thinking about it. Do not read it through to start with. Do not try to correct it. Leave it just as it is.

• Go back once more to that place of failure. What people do you find there? What relationship do you have with these people? Do you dominate them? Do they dominate you? Or are you equals?

• What relationship do you have with your horse? With horses in general. What makes your relationships with horses fail? Can you see your relationships as they are and change them from there? Can you feel the strength which is hidden behind your failure?

Step Nine
Catastrophe

• Remember the goal you set for yourself in step four of the journey? Go through your notes and ask yourself what has become of your goal.

• What motif or mantra was supposed to accompany you on your way? And what has actually happened on your journey?

• Is there a point that hurts? A shadow you cannot jump over?

• Light a torch. And go through your life. Find all that is dried up and will burn easily. Find all that is unclear, vague, shaky, everything that has long been shrivelling up. And set fire to it! Fan the great fire. Then go to the stable and do something quite simple with your horse.

• Write down all the spells that you have cast on yourself.

I am not …

I will never …

I am not allowed to …

I cannot …

I am too …

I have no right to …

Never …

• Write everything down that prevents you from immediately following your dreams, now at this moment. And then swear. Put a curse on this rubbish.

- Which are the predators that threaten your life? Ask your body. Ask your horse. Name your predator and feel its energy. The sensitive animal at your side will tell you how far you have to flee. Find a safe place.

- In the middle of the storm, where are your signposts? Can you keep a cool head and ask the way from someone who knows? Can you find the information that shows the way out of the storm?

- Can you feel that something is moving, even if from the outside it seems to be standing still?

- Can you find the true connection to yourself in the middle of the catastrophe? Can you find the gateway? Name it.

Step Ten
The Climax

• What is happening in your life at this very moment? What are you sad about, impatient, happy, excited, annoyed, hurt? The feeling that you experience at this moment is your gateway. No matter how you are feeling right now, this is the point from which you set off.

• What do you believe in? What is your own completely private belief, valid only for you? The belief in the immortality of the soul, in God, in karma, reincarnation, beauty? You are free to believe in what gives you courage and fulfilment. Write your vision down or paint it.

• Can you find the steppes within yourself? The place of courage? The place where your view is unrestricted and you can survey the whole landscape? That elevated point from which you find insight, security, wisdom? What do you see there?

Step Eleven
Conclusion

• What has the end of your journey brought you to? Do you remember setting off? Your weakness? Your strength? How have these two qualities influenced your route? Can you see the weakness in your strength and the strength in your weakness? Can you see how they both belong together? Have you found your centre? Your name? Look for an image or an object that stands for the conclusion of your journey? A fare-well gift.

• Which place have you reached that you have never been to before? Which taboo, which inner no-go area have you transcended?

• Take a sheet of paper, draw what comes to mind and study the drawing. When you concentrate on it for a while, it will start to talk to you. If you ask an animal to help you read the drawing, you will get interesting information. This is one example amongst many. Find your own exercises, your own channels.

• Go out into life, heroine, and connect.

Bibliography

Andrews, Ted	*Animal-Speak: The Spiritual & Magical Powers of Creatures Great and Small*
Aron, Elaine N.	*The Highly Sensitive Person*
Beck, Martha	*Finding Your Way in a Wild New World*
Campbell, Joseph	*The Power of Myth*
Coelho, Paolo	*The Alchemist*
Cunningham, Keith	*The Soul of Screenwriting*
Dass, Ram	*Journey of Awakening: A Meditator's Guidebook*
Dietmann, Ulrike	*The Medicine Horse*
Grof, Stanislav	*The Adventure of Self Discovery*
Grof, S. & Christina	*Spiritual Emergency: When Personal Transformation Becomes a Crisis*
Hesse, Hermann	*Siddartha*
Villoldo, Alberto	*The Shaman's Way of Healing*
Carl Gustav	*Psychology and Alchemy*
Kidd, Sue Monk.	*When the Heart Waits: Spiritual Direction for Life's Sacred Questions*
Kohanov, Linda	*The Tao of Equus: A Woman's Journey of Healing and Transformation Through the Way of the Horse*
Kohanov, Linda	*Riding Between the Worlds: Expanding our Potential Through the Way of the Horse*

Kohanov, Linda	*The Way of the Horse: Equine Archetypes for Self-Discovery. A Book of Exploration and 40 Cards*
Lao-Tse	*Tao Te Ching*
McLaren, Karla	*Emotional Genius: Discovering the Deepest Language of the Soul*
McLaren, Karla	*Becoming an Empath*
Myss, Caroline	*Sacred Contracts*
O'Donohue, John	*Anam Cara – A book of Celtic Wisdom*
Rosenberg, Shelley	*My Horses, My Healers*
Sams & Carson	*Medicine Cards*
Stromberg, Tony	*Spirit Horses* (Photographs)
Tolle, Eckhart	*The Power of Now: A Guide to Spiritual Enlightenment*
Tolle, Eckhart	*A New Earth: Awakening to Your Life's Purpose*
DVD	*The Path of the Horse* (Stormy May Productions)

Biography

Ulrike Dietmann, born in 1961, studied at Berlin University of the Arts. She is author of numerous fiction and non-fiction books. Horses have been her companions since childhood.

The author has completed her training as Epona Advanced Instructor with Linda Kohanov, USA, and operates her own business of equine facilitated learning in Germany.

She teaches the Hero's Journey with Horses in Germany and international. She lives in Southern Germany with her family. Visit her Web Site: www.spirithorse.info

Thank you to my brothers and sisters who walk on this earth

I wrote this book in 2009 and it was published in German the same year. It was a bestseller in the spiritual field and I received many very touching e-mails from readers. 2012 it was published in French and now in English language. Working with horses and humans continues to change my life every day in many dimensions. It is also very fulfilling to see that the evolving consciousness that humans and horses share has become an impressive reality around the globe.

First and foremost I wish to express my sincere gratitude to Linda Kohanov, brilliant author and visionary, who–like no other–has revealed for us access to the depth of the human soul, along the seam where it melds with the wisdom and the soul of horses. Linda Kohanov and her team have been and continue to be my teachers and wonderful colleagues.

Deep gratitude goes to the two translators, Andrea Zwingelberg-Woods und her husband Roy Woods. I love their translation and am most impressed by how they have especially succeeded in translating the spirit of the book.

Many thanks, also, to Synnove Bakke, who invited me to Norway to lead a workshop on the Hero's Journey and–amongst other things – encouraged me to have the book translated into English.

Thank you to the teachers, classmates and colleagues that have shared my path: Carol Roush, dear friend, soul mate, and most wonderful colleague, Sharon Bringleson, my mentor, who is teaching me about the deep mysteries of being with horses, Mary-Louise

Gould, who I have the honour to know, Shelley Rosenberg, who encouraged me to be a real horse woman. Yvonne Monahan, Ireland, who introduced the Epona Approach to me. My fellow travellers on the great journey: Rosie Withey, Kath Garnett, Ingrid Krimmer, Caroline Morgan, Dellarose Baevski, Marianne Borg, Sandra Sell-Lee, Julie Bridge, Dale Carnathan, Carol Hammon-Paulson, Lauren Loos, Larney Otis, Ineke Rietveld, Astrid Dielhenn, Uschi Schröder, Heike Gäßler, Eva Reifler, Natalie Frey, Ira Rienecker, Ulrike Mayer, Elke Wedig and many others.

Thank you also to Kim McElroy whose horse portraits are breathtaking. To visit her website *spiritofhorse.com* is a magical experience and twice already I came back with just the right cover for a book. I thank Kim also for her support in introducing the book to a bigger audience.

Furthermore I wish to thank Isabella Sonntag, who published the German version of my book and the German editions of books by Linda Kohanov. With her publishing company Wu Wei Verlag, www. wu-wei-verlag.de, she gives a voice to the horses, that is heard all over the world.

Many splendid horses have been my teachers, above all my Arab soul mate Tinnia Alwirathe Jeszna, who constantly surprises me with her gentleness, her inspirations and her unconditional love.

The Epona Approach created by Linda Kohanov has had profound resonance in Germany and France in the last years and continues to unfold in magnificent ways. These days I teach the Hero's Journey with Horses in workshops and as an apprenticeship. Through my work I meet the most wonderful people and I have experienced many miracles. The peaceful, self-confident message of horses touches an ancient longing in us humans. It reawakens an ancient dream we have not forgotten. At the present moment this dream seems to be returning with full force. What is happening awakens deep gratitude in everyone who gets in touch with it. Therefore I thank all my brothers and sisters who form part of the great family of living beings on this planet.

Kirchheim, 28.11. 2012

Ulrike Dietmann

Best friends and pathfinders: Tinnia and Ulrike

To contact me, please visit my website www.spirithorse.info. Reader's feedback always makes me happy!

Zeitfracht Medien GmbH
Ferdinand-Jühlke-Straße 7
99095 Erfurt, Deutschland
produktsicherheit@kolibri360.de